Contents

Foreward

Why Price Hill Boy?

Well, it's like this…

In my 60 odd years on the planet I've had the opportunity to experience a lot. As a performer, I've had the opportunity to work with incredibly talented people. As a professional, I've traveled all over the world. As a person, I've met amazing people from all walks of life. Do I think that's because I am somehow special?

Nope.

I think that what I am is a very ordinary person who has been presented with some extraordinary opportunities. One of the talents I think I have is the ability, and tendency, to say "Yes".

Bob, want to move to California? ….Yes.

Bob, want to sing on cruise ships?…Yes

Bob, want to join the circus?…. and so on.

I've had people say to me "You should write a book about your life". I've resisted the idea. I didn't know if it would be all that fascinating. I still don't. But what I'm going to do is put together stories. Kinda like my blog site. Yes, I have a blog site. It's called "Practically Well". (Practicallywell.net, if you must know) I blog about health & wellness, and all of the knowledge, pseudo-knowledge and just plain bull associated with it, from the perspective of a middle aged guy from the midwest. I started that in October of 2018. and in the last 5 1/2 years have generated about 42 followers.

42.

That's not an influencer. Or a mini-influencer. Or a micro-influencer. That's more of a self-influencer. I do it for me. As sort of a creative outlet.

I've also written plays. And actually had a few of them produced in both L.A. and New York. I actually had a short video of a piece I wrote called "Black & Blue", about the relationship between law enforcement and the African American community, accepted as a part of the "Queens Underground Black & Brown Film Festival " in 2021. I was honored and amused in equal measure.

The point being I've done some writing.

So I'm going to stick to the blog template. I'll share stories about, simply put, experiences. Some hopefully funny, some maybe a bit more serious. We'll see how this goes. When it comes to other folks who are involved in these stories, I'm going to change names slightly and minimize their inclusion here. I don't think people should just be thrown in to this little project without their consent. And if it's something really heinous, I simply won't include it. I can't think of what that might be, but just saying.

And oh, that's right, not everyone knows what a "Price Hill" is. Price Hill is the neighborhood I grew up in. In my day, my day being the 60's and 70s, Price Hill was a middle / lower middle class neighborhood on the west side of Cincinnati, Ohio. And I have a lot of Price Hill still in me. 40+ years of world travel and performing arts hasn't completely removed it. For which I'm glad. My Price Hill attitude has saved my sorry butt more than once. But I think that's a story to be told in the ensuing pages....

So. I think that's enough prep. I hope you enjoy.

Cheers,

Bob

1-Growing up Price Hill

Cincinnati is a town like Korea is a country. Or Germany before the wall came down. East side & West side.

The East side is posh. Wine, pickleball, golf…

West side is working class. Beer, softball, bowling, bars…

Price Hill is the epitome of west side. Pete Rose, may he rest in peace, was from Price Hill. And he was a perfect example of a west sider. He was never the biggest, the fastest or the strongest. But Pete outfought & outworked everyone on his way to having the most hits in major league baseball history. And if you don't think he belongs in the Baseball Hall of Fame, you're nuts. Starting with Ty Cobb, there are cheaters, juicers, womanizers and flat out criminals who have places in Cooperstown. But see, that's the other part of Pete being a Price Hill guy. He wasn't going to admit he was wrong. He said exactly what was on his mind without regard for who it offended or pissed off.

If you want to get a tough job done, hire a Price Hill guy. If you want somebody who is pretty, cultured and politically correct, look somewhere else. Are there exceptions, sure. Folks would probably call me atypical for a Price Hill guy, if for no other reason than I just used the term "atypical". But in general, that's the different between east side and west side. Being brought up in Price Hill on the west side in the 60s and 70s….

…you played outside. "Go outside and play"was something you heard from Mom or Dad on a regular basis. We played baseball & football on the street, and basketball in the driveway of houses that had hoops. Soccer was something exotic. We never even saw it, much less played it. We played "Kick the Can" at night until the streetlights came on and you'd hear mothers yelling " Robert Michael Joseph Tully (or fill in the name), get in here now!"

…If you messed around at school, you got hit. It could be an openhanded smack in the head, a ruler across the knuckles or a paddling. And parents were aright with it. In many cases you'd get punished at school, then again at home.

…We had block parties and festivals. The first time I ever sang on a stage was at a street party on Francis Ave. I sang a duet of "Jackson"with a neighborhood girl. We set up booths and strung lights and played music on speakers in front yards.

…People sat on their porches in the evening and neighbors would come over and chat.

…lemonade stands, kool-aide stands, bake sales.

…Sundays were for church, and if you were lucky you'd stop at the Butterkist bakery on the way home and pick up donuts or a tea ring. If you don't know what a tea ring is, it's basically a big pastry shaped like a ring that you cut up and shared. SO good.

…You could still take your jug and get it filled with beer at the local pony keg.

…Milkmen. You could tell him what you wanted and he would leave it in the box on the porch.

Was it a better time?

Apples and oranges. That's the best answer I can give. I knew people who were crippled by polio, prejudice was commonplace, we grew up largely ignorant of other people, cultures religions, etc. But it was the time I grew up in.

On weekend nights, my parents, grandparents, aunts & uncles would get together to play cards. We'd put the extra "leaf" into the dining room table to make it bigger and put on the folding vinyl cover. They were all drinking & smoking cigarettes and cigars and the room was thick with smoke. We'd be watching, crawling under the table and getting the adults drinks when they ran out. And they'd give us an occasional puff of a cigarette or a drink of beer. Of course we'd also sneak a smoke or a drink of booze and get smacked if we got busted.

On weekends, we'd get up early to clean the house and cut the grass. Dad was very particular about how the grass was cut, the edges were trimmed, the porch and stairs and sidewalk were swept and hosed down.It was a matter of neighborhood pride. Yeah, we had that too.

I used to cut my grandparent's grass. My father's folks. It put a few bucks in my pocket. One day I was cutting their front lawn while the next door neighbor was washing his car. He was, like many guys back then, very particular about his car. That's probably still true today, but back then it was more of a hands on type of thing. You washed, dried, waxed and detailed it in your driveway.

Well, just about the time he was waxing, I was cutting the front lawn. I didn't see the dirt patch. Grandpa's grass was usually very even and green, etc. But that day there was a tiny mound of dirt, raised just enough for the blades of the lawnmower to blast it into a small, but very discernible dirt cloud. And which way was the wind blowing…?

The neighbor and I both watched that cloud waft towards his car. There was no time to get in the car, start it and move out the way. There was no way for me to huff and puff the dirt cloud off course. We both just watched it slowly and inexorably drift up to and onto his freshly washed and waxed car. I was frozen, standing behind the still running lawnmower. He stood there for a moment, staring daggers at me, then threw his rag down and stomped back into his house. We never said a word to each other the whole time, nor did we ever speak again, though I cut my grandparents grass for years after….

…but I digress…

Oh, and btw, digressions are a part of me as a writer. I call myself out on them, and try to keep them short & to the point, but love them or hate them, there they are. Just being transparent, as the kids say nowadays.

For me, growing up Price Hill was;

- Singing weddings at St. Williams and lining up to get a quarter, which you then spent over at the Taffy House or Miles Beresford's for penny candy.

- Disputes being resolved in "the Hollow" after school, with fists, and usually in about 30 seconds or less.

- Playgrounds which were blacktop or concrete, with metal monkey bars, teeter-totters, full contact dodge-ball. I once had my nose bloodied and my glasses destroyed by a dodgeball.

- Family parties complete with lawn jarts, smoking, drinking and on July 4th, huge amounts of illicit fireworks, set off by the same people who had been indulging in the smoking and drinking, with the occasional life threatening results that you would expect.

- Paul Dixon, Bob Braun, Ruth Lyons & Nick Clooney.

- Getting sent to the IGA for groceries, and trying to figure out how to sneak a snack or pop into the purchase without getting busted.

- Coney Island, then Kings Island.

- Crosley field, then Riverfront coliseum.

- The Royals, til they left. The Bengals, when they first started, the Reds, always.

- Do I miss those days? I do, in some ways. I think as kids raised there and then, we were thrown into the deep end of social interaction. I was, am, and will always be something of a loner but I think without that forced interaction I wouldn't have learned how to cope with people as much as I have. I think being raised in Price Hill has given me a very pragmatic view of life, which theater, Los Angeles, world travel and mixing with the rich, famous and self important hasn't been able to get rid of. I value that very much.

Have I changed? Haven't we all? And yes, all of the experiences, places, people, cultures, food, music, etc, etc, etc have definitely had an influence on me. A welcome influence, from my perspective. But at my core, I think that growing up in Price Hill has grounded me. Not geographically, certainly. But as regards basic values, how I see and interact with people, how I treat the 16 year old waitress at Frisch's and the 70 year old greeter at La Rosa's. Or the 16 year old fruit seller in Phuket and the 70 year old train attendant in Japan.

We're all different. And we're all the same. And I think that's one of the things that Price Hill has given me.

That's a pretty cool gift.

Me, impersonating a baseball player..

2-Fat & Fit

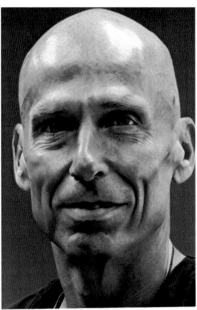

No cheekbones   Cheekbones

I was fat.

Significantly fat. For a while. I wasn't fat as a small child. But right around 13, right around puberty, I turned to food.

I've said before, and truly believe, that had there been such a thing as a "spectrum" when I was young, I would have been on it. I was painfully awkward in social situations.

I played some team sports, which helped. Team sports worked for the same reason theater works. It's a group of people working towards a goal. I don't have to engage in small talk. I don't have to be clever or charming. We are there to accomplish something and the collaborative work makes interaction easy. Afterparties and nights out are another thing. And they follow a pattern for me.

I go. I talk to the people I want to talk to. Eventually, conversations devolve into groups, with people speaking over each other, trying to be clever or funny or impressive. I don't want to compete in a social setting. So I stand or sit and watch these people talk to each other. When I was younger I would try to interject myself into these conversations, try to compete. But I don't want to anymore. I'm really not interested in small talk. So I leave.

It's not a sad thing. I'm really good with it. Every once in a great while I connect with someone and get into a conversation. But I'd say at least 90% of the time I hit that point and walk. Sometimes I say goodbye, sometimes I feel like it would be intrusive, so I just hit the exit. Again, I'm not sad, or disappointed. It would be uncomfortable and awkward if I tried to stay. Leaving is much the better option…

…but I digress…

At 13-ish, what took the place of social interaction in my life was food. For me, food was and always has been fun. I enjoy the act of eating , of tasting good food. I don't understand people who say that they forget meals. I have no idea how you do that. When I'm eating lunch, I am planning dinner. And much like fitness is a hard-wired habit in my life now, eating junk food was back then. I ate unhealthy amounts of unhealthy foods because I enjoyed the experience. And I didn't have other interactions. This is not a "poor me"piece. It's a recounting of what happened, of how I got where I got.

I was addicted to chips & dip. It got to the point where my family would prepare additional chips and dip, knowing that I would camp out in front of it and chow down. And the heavier I got, the less active I got. And the less active I got, the heavier I got.

You see the cycle.

So I was heavy, and socially awkward. From 13 through my early 20s. Those formative, high school, 1st date, prom years. One of my favorite throw-away lines is that I was a fat kid who sang in the glee club at a Catholic jock school in the late 70's. A certain amount of bullying was almost to be expected. But again I go back to…this is not a "poor me" scenario. I had friends. I think I was more of a "mascot" than anything else. But they were friends with me when there was no reason to be, and I appreciate that.

Then, in my early - mid 20s, something changed.

Don't ask me what or why. There was no "burning bush" moment. No climactic moment when I started chiseling at the wall of the prison cell and a chunk came out..To the best of my recollection, I just decided to run around the block one day. Not even a mile, just around the block. And doing it once became doing it on a regular basis. Then just running became going to the Cincinnati YMCA and working out. And then the diet started.

And folks, I did the diet totally wrong. I did it the way you are not supposed to do it. 1200 calories a day. Working out and sauna-ing until I would black out..The powers that be will tell you that this kind of extreme diet/work out routine will lose the weight, but then it will all come back plus more, eventually. Only it didn't. For some reason, I was the exception to that rule. And I do believe what they say is true in 99% of cases. Just not mine.

That's what took me from 265 lbs to 220, then to 195, then down to 180-ish, by the time I was around 30. And that's where it's stayed since then, more or less. Occasionally I let things go a bit, and then I have to have a quick "come to Jesus" moment and get back on the program for a minute. Basically, I've been lucky enough, and made good enough choices to maintain my weight. And no, I don't think wellness is a number on a scale but for me it's a fairly good road sign.

Then after I got to L.A., I started taking group fitness classes. Then I got asked to get certified and start teaching, which I did. I spent 20 years teaching for 24 Hour Fitness and L.A. Fitness, among others. I even taught at Linda Evans Fitness, which was an all women's gym, which amused me no end. And subsequently, running became a part of my life, which I'll recount in other pieces here.

I still love food. I just have a different, and I think better, relationship with it. I hate the word "moderation", but it probably describes it as well as anything. But I don't think of it as being moderate. I think that as you reduce your food intake, what you think of as a good portion of food changes. My year in Japan changed my concept of portion size completely. When I came back to the States after a year in Japan, I was amazed at the size of American portions.

So, all this to say that I've looked at life through both sides now, to quote Joni Mitchell. And I value the whole experience. I think being fat in a thin world teaches you about people. About prejudice, based on appearance.

And one last thing I want to make perfectly clear.

Fitness is a choice.

I don't think that there is anything inherently better, or more noble, about being fit. You choose how you live your life, and you make choices based on what you want. There are people who are way more fit than I. There are people who don't have any interest in fitness whatsoever. I had a actor friend named Geno. Geno would delight in bringing whatever "meatball hoagie with extra cheese and mayo on the side" he was having for dinner, along with the beer he was washing it down with, eat it in front of me and then tell me he was going outside for an after dinner cigarette. I would tell him "I'm happy to give you a light if you want". I am a great believer in self-determination. What I don't respect is living that life and then getting all regretful and repentant when the cancer, diabetes, etc happens. Yup Brynner did that. And John Matuzak. I don't want to hear it, I want you to have another order of smothered and covered fries and light up your Lucky after you get the diagnosis…

…But I digress…

I think that after being heavy throughout those years, as I was growing up, I will always think of myself that way on some level. Intellectually I know that I am fit, and if anything on the thin side. But somewhere inside I will always carry around that kid who was nicknamed "whale".

And that's a good thing.

Fitness Staff, L.A. Fitness, California 1990-ish

3-Community Theater

"Annie get your Gun". A while ago..

I have a lot to thank community theater for.

Because, as I think I have mentioned, I wasn't exactly fast tracked for success when it comes to performing arts. As a heavy set, socially awkward 20-ish guy who could sing a little, I wasn't exactly overwhelmed with performing opportunities, paid or unpaid. I was given opportunities by people who saw something, or had enough faith to give me a shot.

Of course the 1st one was Dave Allen. This is the one time I am using a real name. Dave is a graduate of CCM, the College-Conservatory of Music in Cincinnati . He took the job as choir director at St. Williams church in Price Hill several years before I joined the boys choir in the late 60's. He also started directing the glee club at Elder High.School in Cincinnati. And today, as of me writing this, 50+ years later, he still holds those positions. That is amazing on many levels. That he has maintained his love of music, teaching, directing and maintained his faith is, to me, an incredible statement . And he has introduced thousands of young people to the performing arts. To most, it gave them a healthy appreciation of the arts. To a few, like yours truly, it became a career and lifetime love affair.

And since my return to Cincinnati, I've gotten the opportunity to re-connect with Dave and the Elder/Seton performing arts community. Dave is in his 80s now, but still has energy and enthusiasm for the work. And, after a rehearsal for a local concert, when I first got back in town, he invited me over to the Crow's Nest for a few beers. Hilarious. And Dave was the first of a number of people who gave me, well, an opportunity.

After high school, community theater continued my education. However, it wasn't love at first sight. In the early 80's I auditioned for a show called "Lorelei" at St James Players in White Oak. This was a small, I mean SMALL theater on the west side of town. And, at 20 something years old, auditioning at a tiny community theatre , I got….nothing.

Not a lead, not the chorus. Nothing. I know performers who have had to turn down paid contracts because they were still in high school. I know young people who have had to be tutored on set. And I couldn't get cast in the chorus. For free.

But this is the moment that I look at as my starting point. Early 20s, not quite good enough to even get cast. And the long, and yeah, winding road from there to here, makes me appreciate the trip. When I look at some of the jobs I have been fortunate enough to book, and some of the opportunities I've had, and the work it has taken to get there, yes, I'll admit it. I'm kinda proud.

And community theater has had a lot to do with that. It was my first acting class. Because, friends, I was NOT a very good actor when I started out. The reason I got roles, really good, leading roles, was simple. I was a guy who could sing. In Cincinnati, Ohio. In the 80s. If I had been a woman, there would have been a dozen other women who could do what I could, and probably act better. But in that time and that place, there weren't a lot of guys who were into performing and had a decent singing voice. So I got cast. And folks, starting out, I absolutely butchered some really good roles…

Frank Butler in "Annie get your Gun"

Fred Graham in "Kiss Me Kate"

Captain Von Trapp in "Sound of Music"

Just to name a few. But, you know what? I learned. I worked with people who were better, and more trained than I was, and I improved. Slowly, sometimes painfully so, I learned. That learning continued through the Los Angeles theater scene, cruise ships, Japan and greatly informed the work I did as a corporate speaker, but it all started in community theater.

I think another thing I can thank community theater for is helping out a painfully awkward young person to get more comfortable socially. The Cincinnati theater community became my family. I partied, worked, dated, and generally lived as a part of this group, and it helped me to develop the social skills that I have. I'm never going to be an extrovert, and I will always embrace my alone time, but having to work with others through the rehearsal & performance process brought me out of a very hard and tight shell.

Since coming back to Cincinnati after 35 years, I have tried reconnecting with the community theater, umm, community. But 35 years is a long time. I moved on with my life and so have other people.

I don't resent this. I've kept in touch with some folks from those days and it's great to see them again, and see where life has taken them. I think it's important to acknowledge where you come from, and the people who have helped you along the way. And I'll always be grateful to the Cincinnati community of theaters, and community theater in general.

Thanks to;

Dave,

Fifi,

Cindy,

Elston,

Denny,

Dave (different Dave)

I appreciate it.

4-Johnny Rosebud

So, it's 1986. I'm still in Cincinnati, working and doing community theater, etc. My former girlfriend, Sandra, has moved to California for her job, and I am dating another girl who's also involved in local theater. Deena is a nice & utterly gorgeous girl, and life is going well in that regard.

My buddy Jerome and I have actually been, without really planning to, paralleling each other as regards dating. When I dated Sandra, he was dating a good friend of hers. Now that I was dating Deena, he was dating another woman, who would eventually become Mrs. Jerome. The two girls we were dating knew each other. Both were active in local performing arts. I think we had double dated with them a time or two. You get the idea.

Jerome's ex had also left town. Life had moved on. It was early February and we were approaching Valentine's Day when Jerome and I got word that both of our ex's were coming back into town and wanted to meet up for dinner, drinks, etc. The date that actually worked for all of us was Valentine's Day itself.

OK, dinner, catch up with some friends, a nice little social interaction, right? Who could possibly have an issue with that?

Hmmm…

Well, Deena could possibly misunderstand the idea of me meeting up with my ex on Valentine's Day. What I don't want is a misunderstanding. And seeing that it's Valentine's Day, Deena could feel like I should be spending it with her. I understand that. But this is my one chance to meet up with Sandra. I can make it up to Deena afterwards, right? So, why create a potential issue by telling her about the meetup?

Yeah, I know. But these were my thoughts, rationalizations, (tomato, tomato) So no, I didn't.

Flash forward to Valentine's Day. As we're heading over to meet the girls at a local restaurant, I ask Jerome, "did you tell MK?" .

"Of course I did. You told Deena, right?"……"right?"

Hmmm.

So, we get to the restaurant, meet up with the girls and proceed to have a nice dinner and catch up session. In the midst of the meal, Johnny Rosebud enters the place.

Who's Johnny Rosebud?

Johnny was a local "personality".He's an older dude who goes around selling roses. You see him on the street, or in local establishments, peddling his flowers. He also gets up with a few local bands from time to time and sings the song "Kansas City". Just a local character.

So Johnny walks in, followed by a local news crew. Cameraman, reporter. You know, that kind of thing. He starts going from table to table, trying to sell his roses. On Valentine's Day. And as we are talking, I can't help but notice that no one is buying a flower. Johnny's got a news crew with him. On Valentine's Day. And nobody is buying a flower.

C'mon now.

Somebody should help a brother out. Those were my honest, well intentioned thoughts at the time. So, they get to our table and I say "Sure, I'll buy a flower." Jerome is looking at me, very directly, but I don't pay this any particular mind. I mean, what else are you going to do, huh? And, given that this is Valentine's Day, and you've just bought a flower from Johnny Rosebud for "your girl", for the sake of the news crew, what's the button, huh? So yeah, I give Sandra the rose. And give her a kiss. Perfect. The news crew thanks me and says "Look for this on the 11 o'clock news tonight".

Cool.

I've helped out Johnny. It's nice moment for the table. And the local broadcast. Win - Win, right? So why is Jerome still intently staring at me?

"Bob, I need to use the Men's room."

"OK " (He's still staring..)

"Oh, yeah, so do I…"

We get up and excuse ourselves.

"Well that was kinda cool, huh?"

"Bob"

"What?"

"The 11 o'clock news"

" What?..........Oh"

"Yeah, oh"

Deena was at home, with her parents, watching the 11 o'clock news that night. I won't say that it ended our relationship right there and then, but I think " undermined the foundations" wouldn't be overstating it.

In the interest of transparency, Sandra was the girl I ended up moving to California to live with, so maybe that relationship wasn't a completely done deal. The positive part of it was that Jerome looked so much better in his girlfriend's eyes. Maybe I helped him in that regard. Maybe he didn't need my help, but I try to find the positive in my life experiences. So sue me.

The lesson?

Honesty is the best policy. Or, you can't fix stupid.

Take your pick.

5-L.A.

So how did I transition from a mid-20s guy working in Cincinnati to the West Coast?

Quickly and randomly, thank you for asking. And there was a woman involved.

Through my early and mid 20's I had flirted with performing arts. In my early 20's I spent a semester at the Cincinnati College-Conservatory of Music. But I wasn't prepared financially, artistically or emotionally to follow through on that, so I ended up getting a "real" job and involving myself in local theater. Which is a story you're already heard.

Then, when I was 26 I went back to school. To Northern Kentucky University. Again for performing arts. And I renewed a relationship with a girl who I had dated before she left for California. Yeah, that one. Sandra was going to return to Cincinnati to take a job with a local company. She was going to drive from California to Cincinnati. Sandra was a smart woman. But she was also a 5'2" 27 year old women driving across the country, alone. So we decided I would fly to Modesto and ride back with her. It's not that I'm much of a bodyguard, but I look like I might be.

So I fly out to Modesto and am greeted with a story. It seems that Sandra's boss, Earnest Gallo (yes, that Earnest Gallo)) offered her a stupid amount of money to stay for another year. At least that was the story I got.

So, as 20 somethings who were in what we perceived to be love at the time, we decided that I should come out to Modesto and stay with her. Sort of try out the living together thing, and the California thing. So I fly back to Cincinnati, load up my beat up Cutlass Supreme, and drive out to start my new life with Sandra in Modesto.

Modesto lasted a year, for both of us. Then we moved to Los Angeles. Actually Glendale, a little suburb just north of DTLA, between Burbank & Pasadena. I got a job with the same company I had worked with in Modesto, Sandra went back to college to study voice. That lasted about another year. Then Sandra & I went our separate ways. I would say amicably, but that would be overstating it. She went on to get her degree and, last I heard, entered academia. I became a broke actor for a while. At least until 1993 when I got an offer from Norwegian Cruise lines.

But I'm getting ahead of myself. One story at a time, Bob.

6-John Raitt

It was early days in Los Angeles . Sandra and I had a small apartment in Glendale. I was working at an office and Sandra was going to school for voice. That was a situation that eventually came to a head, but you've already heard that story. There was, at that time, a Glendale Music Theater. Glendale is a rather affluent suburb of L.A., situated between Burbank and Pasadena. I had performed the role of Captain Von Trapp in their previous year's production of "The Sound of Music". They were having auditions for their next show, which was "South Pacific". And John Raitt was doing the role of Emile Debeque.

If you don't know who John Raitt is, I'm going to guess that you don't really follow musical theater. John was an old school Broadway star. He starred in "Oklahoma","Carousel" and many other productions on Broadway. He starred with Doris Day in the movie "The Pajama Game". And, just btw, he was also the father of one Bonnie Raitt, the amazing blues artist. So I wanted the role of Lt. Cable, the young love interest in the show.

Hey, I was 29. I had hair. Yes, I was young once.

So, I go to the auditions. My friends who were running the audition told me that there hadn't been any amazing auditions for the role I wanted. Cool. They were bringing us into the theater in groups of 3 to audition, and so I get called in with 2 other guys. One is an older gentleman who is auditioning for one of the character roles, and he gets called up on stage first. There are 5-6 people in the house. Director, choreographer, music director, etc.

As the first guy is doing his thing, the young guy next to me introduces himself;

"Hey, I'm Tony"

"Hey Tony, Bob"

Tony asks "You ever done this kinda stuff before? I'm kinda new to this. I'm just here because my roommate says I might be good for the young guy, Lt. Cable?"

Very young. Thick Boston accent.

I ask Tony if he's done much acting work. He replies "No, God no. But I sing."

Bless his little heart. But you can tell he's this good-hearted dude. I already like Tony. Also, I'm not sensing he's a real threat, casting wise. So I ask him what he's going to sing and he tells me he's going to do "Bring Him Home", from Les Miserables.

I really want to tell Tony not to. He's young . He's inexperienced. "Bring Him Home" is a difficult, and crazy high, song. I don't want him to be awful. But as I'm trying to figure out how to tell him this, he gets called to the stage. Oh well. My intentions were good. Afterwards maybe I can let him down easy and give him some tips, advice, etc.

You already know where this is going, right?

So he gets up, gives the accompanist the sheet music, and addresses the table, the music starts …and the voice of God comes out of Tony's mouth. The tone, the inflection, the effortless high notes…

Until this moment the producers table had been half listening while they looked at resumes, talked among themselves, etc. When Tony starts they all stop and look up, more or less transfixed, then look at his resume, look back up, riveted. We were supposed to get 16 measures but Tony sang the whole song. It wasn't even a question. Nobody wanted him to stop. Even I wanted to hear the whole thing. I couldn't even be angry. He was a nice guy. With an amazing instrument.

So he finishes. They have questions. And of course they ask him to stay. A few of them actually are still talking to him when they call;

"Next, Mr…Tully?

Damn.

All I could think of is. "OK, just do what you do. Sing the song & get to the callback. Tony said he wasn't an actor. So just sing the song". Which I do. They aren't transfixed. They aren't riveted, but they do ask me to stay for the movement call. BTW, "movement call" is what they call a dance audition when they don't want to scare actors/singers like me. But again, a different story.

We get to the movement call. There are about a dozen of us, auditioning for various roles. They teach the combination. Nothing too crazy. I'm not great but not terrible. Tony's with me in the movement call and he's really nervous. When they call on us to do the combination in groups of three , Tony says " I'm sorry, I just can't" and starts to walk off the stage. Half of the production team fall all over each other to stop him.

"It's all right, the movement isn't really important to the role. Just stay. we'd like to read you afterwards.."

Hmm..

So after the movement call, they ask 3 of us to stay and read. Tony, me and another guy. OK, cool, because this is kinda what I do. If I'm still here, then I may have a good shot. Tony is inexperienced as an actor. He reads the lines but that's about it.The other guy, alright, but nothing special and the voice wasn't amazing. So the producers ask us to wait. They talk for a while. They release the other guy and ask Tony and I to stick around.

They start with Tony. "Young man, you have an amazing voice and we'd love for you to be a part of this production. It would be a great opportunity for you…blah, blah, blah"… You know, all that stuff.

So I'm thinking "Wow. After all of this, things have worked out. Lt. Cable, opposite John Raitt. This is life achievement type stuff. L.A. is really going well so far…etc. Then they turn to me. "Bob, we like you a lot in this role. Just as much as the person we're going to cast. We'd really like you to be a part of this production and understudy the role of Lt. Cable."

Tony is still there. And we are both looking at each other. And looking around for the "person they are going to cast". Because he isn't here. He wasn't at the audition. Or the movement call. Or the reading.

So I go ahead and ask the question. "Who is the person you are casting?".

"Oh, he couldn't be here , but we had a separate call to accommodate him."

And the "person" turns out to be …..the director's boyfriend.

Welcome to L.A.

Tony and I both did the show. We were good friends for a while. I dated his co-worker at a great little restaurant in Pasadena called "Birdie's" that had great muffins. The restaurant, not the co-worker. I went to see Tony front a rock band at the Viper Room in Hollywood. The boy could just flat out sing. That's not the only time I got to experience the "vagaries" of the casting process. But it was the first.

But I did get to say hi to Bonnie on opening night.

So there was that.

7-Knotts & Joe

Dakota Dan & Cameo Kate, Knotts Berry Farm

I worked at Knotts Berry Farm on & off for about 7 years. Knotts is located in Buena Park, Ca., about 4-5 miles from Disneyland. And it is to Disneyland what Lesourdsville Lake is to Kings Island. A reference you will get if you're from Cincinnati. If not, try the term "red-headed stepchild".

The cool thing for me about Knotts was that it was a daytime performing gig, which wasn't very common. So I could work there during the day and then go do another show in the evenings. The pay wasn't great, but it was pay.

The primary role I had at Knotts was "Dakota Dan" in the park's Calico Saloon show, a 20 min. song & dance show that we performed 5 times a day . The cast consisted of Dan, Cameo Kate, a piano player named "Fingers" and, occasionally 2 dancers, depending on the time of year. I also did the Christmas shows at Knotts, in their Bird Cage Theater. We would do short versions of "The Gift of the Magi" and "A Christmas Carol". The casts of those shows were some great veteran actors and the shows there were really well done. Steve Martin actually worked at the Bird Cage way back in the day. The Calico saloon show was very loose and subject to alteration, depending on whether or not park management was around.

There were several performers for every role, since we did shows 7 days a week, and again I got to work with some fun, talented people. But one of my favorite people in the Saloon was not a performer, per se.

Joe was one of the bartenders in the Saloon, serving soda, sarsaparilla and snacks to the park patrons. He was an older gentlemen, in his 80's when I worked with him. A small, skinny, wizened guy. Like Knotts had called Central Casting and asked for a perfect old west saloon bartender. You get the idea.

A word about comedy timing. Comedy is hard. Comedy timing, the ability to deliver a punch time at the right time, in the right way, is a real skill. Great timing can make an unfunny bit funny. Bad timing can kill comedy gold.

Joe was born with it.

Joe was once having a discussion with the piano player between shows. The piano player's wife was about to have a child and at that time there was some controversy about whether or not male children should be circumcised. We went back and forth about it in the green room until it was time for the show.

About halfway through the show, I catch Joe out of the corner of my eye. The stage was located up and behind the bar, so we could look down and see the bartender. Joe had a whole pickle in his hand, which was a snack which they sold in the bar. He then picked up a knife and proceeded to slowly and deliberately perform a bris on the pickle, occasionally taking a quick look up to the piano player.

Pure. Comedy. Gold.

My regular routine with Joe happened when I was singing a classic old song to Kate, "I can't give you anything but Love". In case you're not familiar, here are a few lines;

"I can't give you anything but Love, baby..

That's the only thing I've plenty of, baby…"

Well the word "baby", became Joe's line. He didn't sing it so much as talk/sing/yell it out, while to the audience he was seemingly occupied with whatever else he was doing behind the bar. Then, at the end of the song, where there is one more, final "Baby", Joe would wait, as if he had forgotten. I would prompt him by yelling "Joe!" once or twice before he would deliver the final line. Again, only funny because Joe was funny.

Funny to the audience, hilarious to us, and just something that was created because of his beautiful timing. Management didn't even mind. It was just too good.

One day, between shows, the cast was talking in the green room and Joe came down. It didn't happen very often, but Joe was always welcome. The conversation somehow got around to Joe's past and he shared with us that he had served in Europe during World War 2. He had been part of the allied advance into Germany itself. He talked about how, during the last days of the war, they would often capture German soldiers. Some surrendered, some captured during battles.

"Yeah, there were lots of prisoners. We'd have to take them in, but we'd check them first. If they had the "SS" tattoo. Ya know, that kinda lightning looking "ZZ" kinda tattoo, we'd just shoot them then and there, because we knew the SS soldiers would probably try to kill us if they had the chance....Well, gotta get back to the bar. That Sarsaparilla won't sell itself." (or something like that).

We all just sat there for a minute. Joe, this little old grandfather with beautiful comedy timing and a heart of gold.

It didn't change the way I felt about Joe. But it made me realize that there was more to him than this funny, jovial man. Joe was always upbeat, always positive. I never heard him utter a mean or cruel word. Maybe he had a different perspective on life. I lost track of Joe after I left L.A. for ships. He passed while I was away. But never from my thoughts.

And fond memories.

8-Celebrity

1776 Long Beach CLO. Try to find me & my white wig…

I think celebrity is a kind of drug. A very addictive drug. And once most people gain just a little bit of it, they will do anything to keep it. It's the only reason I can think of for some of the"stuff"on television these days. Reality shows, stars hawking everything under the sun, celebrity boxing, There are a few people who have walked away from stardom, but they are few and far between. They are usually super successful people who take their celebrity for granted. The vast majority fight tooth & nail to retain that notoriety.

I have worked with celebrities from time to time. I did a production of "1776" in Long Beach, Ca. with Dean Jones and an entire cast of character actors whose faces you would know if not their names. I actually didn't even go to the callback for the show. Just prior to this audition, I had been called back for 4-5 jobs and not gotten cast, so I had scheduled a vacation back to Cincinnati. Days before I left, I went to the 1776 audition. It went alright, but then they called and asked me to attend a callback that was 3 days after I was scheduled to leave for Ohio. I thought "I'm not skipping a vacation to go to a callback that will probably not pan out anyway"so I politely declined and got on the plane. 5 days later I get a call while I'm home in Cincinnati.

"Robert?"

"Yeah, this is Bob".

"Robert, this is (whomever) with casting for Long Beach Civic . We'd like to offer you the role of Joseph Hewes in our production of "1776".

FYI, The role of Joseph Hewes is probably the least significant role in the show, and I had actually played it in a high school production in 1976. That didn't bother me, but I was curious …

"Umm thank you. I'm happy to accept but I have to ask. Why are you offering me a role when I didn't come to your callbacks?"

What followed was a brief session of lie-telling, about how they were so impressed with my initial audition that they felt like I was the best choice even though I wasn't at the callback. What I eventually found out was that almost all of the name actors they had cast were tenors. They needed a big baritone voice to fill out the choral singing. That's why I was there. Luckily, I'm not proud. A paying gig is a paying gig.

I was the only non-union actor in the show. Some of the folks were friendly, some not so much. Dean didn't say much, but was kind enough. One of the other cast members , Rutledge from South Carolina, was Ray Benson, at that time the husband of Jody Benson, of "The Little Mermaid" fame.She was sweet and friendly when we met at a cast party.

I also worked with Elaine Stritch the following year at the same theater's production of "Pal Joey". In case you don't know who that is, Elaine is Broadway royalty. Most of the cast were in awe of her. Dixie Carter, from the TV series "Designing Women", was also in the cast. I didn't audition for that show either, but they called me in to fill out the chorus. Another paying gig. Cool. Elaine was just as advertised; crusty, coarse and funny as hell. Dixie was pleasant and I literally almost ran into her husband, Hal Holbrook, while coming offstage during a performance. He looked at me and said "You kids are just marvelous!". I wasn't so much in awe of Elaine, but I've always been a huge Hal Holbrook fan, so my response was gob-smacked silence and then a mumbled "uh, thank you.."

Who I am NOT a fan of was the director of the show. He was a former comedian named David S. I used to see him on the Tonight show and other shows when I was younger. I had no big reaction to finding out he was directing other than "Hmm, didn't know he did that". I never thought he was incredibly funny, but I didn't think much more of it.

Then one day at rehearsal we were blocking a group scene. My character was entering a big party with my "wife". David told everyone to be interacting, chatting, etc as they entered the scene. I knew I had a body mic on so I wanted to know if we should actually talk or pantomime, so I said. "Excuse me David, should we actually be talking?", or something like that.

David stopped, looked at me, and then went on as if I hadn't spoken. A few minutes later an assistant director came up to me and said "Please don't address David directly. If you have questions, just come to me". I get it. I'm not a big deal here. I'm not even in the union. But I can't even talk to the director of the show?

I was pissed. Angry. Furious even. I wish I could tell you I called David a stuck up jerk and walked off the show. But I was a broke actor. It was a gig. But David S., the former comedian and sometimes director, is also a jerk .

At least in my book.

In my corporate job I got to meet Marta, the Brazilian soccer star. We actually had a chat about living in Redondo beach and sushi places before some "media people" ushered her away. Nice, nice lady. And one of the funniest compliments I ever received was from Gabby Reese, the volleyball player, again through my corporate gig. I had given her a tour of the facility and was dropping her in the meeting room with our execs. As I was leaving she said;

"Did I hear you were 55?"

"Yeah, 55"

"You're not married, are you?"

"Nope"

"No kids?"

"None"

"That explains it"

I've found that real major celebs tend to be relaxed and cool people. The hangers on and wanna-bes tend to be the ones with the attitudes.

...and Gabby Reece thinks I look good for my age.

Hells yeah.

9-Curtain Call

There is an old saying that is used to scare prospective performers. It goes something like this;

If you weren't the best singer/actor/dancer in your grade school or high school or college, just forget about doing it as a living.

Well, I wasn't. In any of them. And that pattern has followed me throughout my performing life. There are very few times when I would have even considered myself the strongest performer in any show I have been in. I'm not a very talented person. What I am now, after 40 years of working at it, is skilled. Talent is a gift from God. Or genetic, if the idea of a deity offends you. Skill is something you attain by work and practice. Community theater started my education in real, hands on performing. Where I got my post-graduate work in, if you will, was the Curtain Call.

The Curtain Call was a dinner theater in Orange county. When I started working there in 1989 we did 7 shows a week. Tuesday through Sunday, with 2 shows on Sunday. The shows would run anywhere from 2 months to, honest, I swear, we did a 9 month run of "The Sound of Music". In the interest of transparency, I only did 6 months of that run. Why 9 months? Because the audiences came to see it. Simple economics.

John, the artistic director, took a lot of criticism for running the old, reliable, Rogers & Hammerstein classics. His response?

"It's what sells".

Kinda hard to argue with that logic. Sometimes I think actors get that twisted. They think that theaters should do shows that appeal to them. But by and large, actors don't pay to attend theater. Audiences do. Actors GET paid to do theater.

John would occasionally program some edgy stuff. Not EDGY edgy, but he would put a "Cabaret"or "Zorba" in a season. And we would play to half houses. Or less. Then we'd go back to "Oklahoma"and pack the house. You see, John was running a business. It wasn't supported by "viewers like you", to borrow a phrase from PBS. Theaters that do edgy material are almost always subsidized by local businesses or government, etc. The Curtain Call was basically running on paid attendance.

Actors would also complain about what John paid. John's response?

"I pay what I can pay. You knew what I was paying when you walked in the door. If you really don't like it, don't work here." Again, it was a business.

I got introduced to the Curtain Call when my then girlfriend got hired to play Sally Bowles in "Cabaret". Halfway through the production they lost an actor and she told John that her boyfriend was an actor looking for work. And that is how I get work as an actor more often than not. Not through the front door. Not because "Oh my God he's so talented". It's more like. "Our lead actor took a cruise ship contract and gave us a week's notice. We need a warm body that can speak lines". Yup, through necessity. Through the back door. That's how I get in. Wherever I can fit in.

So, "Cabaret" became "The Music Man" became "Camelot" and so forth to the tune of 26 productions. At 3-5 months a shot. Not all of them were 7 shows a week. they went to a 5 show week towards the end of my time there. But if you do the math, that's a lot of performances.

And I believe that's how you find out whether you actually like acting. Not whether you like to hang around with artistic types or go to the parties or live the lifestyle. On a Wednesday night, 2 months into a 4 month run, when you're playing to half a house and you're doing the 3rd Nazi from the left. That's when you find out if you actually love performing itself. Rain or shine. Sick or well. Excited or bored. Broke or broken up with. Whatever else was going on in your life, you were there when the curtain went up. When the bell rang you toed the line. It was boot camp. For actors.And I learned.

I learned theater self defense. I was playing the King in a production of "The King & I" (yes, back then Irish guys from Ohio got cast as Asian monarchs. Get over it). The woman who played Anna was much more skilled than I was at the time. Early on we had a brief fling. It didn't work out. So she took that out on me. On stage. I regularly got my butt kicked, theatrically. Lines cut off, upstaged, basically anything you could think of.

So I learned to defend myself. And I learned how to cover when things went wrong. I learned how to work with amazing actors by listening to them and watching how they worked. I learned how to deal with actors who didn't give a crap, who were "saving themselves for Broadway" or whatever they called it.

I've taken acting classes. Some were valuable, some not. But where I really learned how to act was on the stage of the Curtain Call theater.

They were also my first theater family in Southern California. Early on, during a production of "Oklahoma", the transmission went out on whatever piece of junk car I was driving at the time. John paid for the repairs. During a production of "The King and I" (not the same one, btw), I got very, very sick. At that point I lived in Glendale, about 40 miles from the theater. John send someone to my home to pick me up, take me to an emergency room and then to his house, where I recovered for the better part of a week. The actors and waiters and staff celebrated holidays, birthdays, New Year's, trips to Vegas, etc. We would do Saturday night shows, party all night, sleep in the parking lot in our cars then shower at the theater in time for the Sunday matinee.

During a production of "Phantom" I would swing on a rope off of a balcony down to the stage at the end of act one. One night the rope broke and I fell into the audience, bounced off the front of the stage and cut both knees wide open on the metal lip of the stage. I limped up the stairs to the stage and finished the act. I went back to the dressing room, we figured out that my knees were just cut up, not broken, bandaged them up and I did the 2nd act. More than a few people advised me to sue the theater.

Nope. I don't sue family.

P.S. I got called out a number of times for my work at Curtain Call. Once I was in a post office in Burbank, waiting in line. A deep voice behind me said "Are you Bob Tully". I turned and looked up at the young man who said it. I'm 6'1" plus a little. But I had to look up. I said "yup" He says " I'm Mikey. I played Kurt in The Sound of Music" with you 10 years ago!" He was very excited. I was amused by the passage of time. When I worked for Norwegian Cruise Lines, they used to have a guest sports personality on board every week. On this particular week it was Mike Pagel, who played quarterback for several NFL teams. I got a message that he wanted to talk to me. OK, the NFL guy wants to talk, sure. So I meet him and he says "I need you to settle a bet I have with my wife. She swears that you were the King in a production of "The King & I" we saw in California when I played for the Rams".

Such is the price of fame.

10-Movies

A Comedy by Hart Monroe

The Wicked Do Prosper

and why shouldn't they?

Ah, what might have been…

Yes, I've done a few movies. No, you won't find them anywhere, unless you have access to my DVD collection, which you don't.

In Los Angeles, making movies is a constant. It's where you go if you want to be in the business. So students are doing their student films. New, fresh young talents are shooting low budget films. People with more money than good sense are branching out into the movie industry. And every once in a while one of these entrepreneurs hits, and a career is born.

So being out in L.A., and being an actor, it was almost inevitable that I would stumble into movies at one point or another. But only a few got as far as actual production, and fewer to a finished product.

One was a horror film shot by my friend Mel's brother. Marcus has done work as a storyboard artist on major films, films you have heard of. And he was kind enough to cast me in a leading role in the film, along with Mel and a few other friends. No, I will not name the film here. But it does exist, and Marcus's work and dedication to the project was amazing. He had an excellent crew as well, other industry professionals. Mel actually got an award at a regional film fest for her work. Me? I got a lot of camera time, bought a mandolin and learned to kinda play it, and got brained with a wooden box that wasn't as "breakaway"as we thought it was.

Also, the day before we started shooting was the day when I, as head coach of a beach camp, tried skim-boarding and removed a fair patch of skin from my face. We actually used my facial sand-blast in the film, and had to replicate it with makeup as it healed.

The other film that I actually wrapped filming on had a working title of "The Wicked Do Prosper". It was a mystery/crime drama. I was cast as a detective, a smallish role. But during shooting the director found out I could juggle. So she asked if I could juggle during the interrogation scene

I am not an accomplished juggler. But I was, at that point, good enough to actually juggle throughout the scene, with only a few drops during the takes. So I became sort of a recurring theme throughout the shoot. And when we had wrapped filming, the producer asked me to come to the Beverly Hills Hotel to shoot the poster for the film. Or, more precisely, the pond in front of the Beverly Hills Hotel. So I stood in the pond, in a suit, and juggled while they shot. Being Beverly Hills, nobody really paid much attention. But one older woman stopped, stared, and approached me after we had finished.

"I know who you are".

" Umm, you do?"

"Yes, You're Ving Rhames".

Strangely enough, I knew that she actually meant Vin Diesel. Wildly inaccurate, but not as off the mark as Ving would have been. So, I took it for the compliment that it was, thanked her and went on my way.

I was really curious about how the movie would turn out. With small independent films, you don't get to see "dailies" or anything like that, so I couldn't wait to see the finished product.

I'm still waiting.

The whole thing disappeared. The production company, the producer, every trace that the film had ever occurred. I wrote emails to the producer. First just asking about progress, then asking for any response, then threatening legal action, though what form that would have taken I had no idea. But no, every trace of the movie and the folks who made it vanished from the face of the earth. The one thing I have, as a souvenir, if you will, was the poster.

Dang, a juggling detective.

It just might have been a hit.

11-Cruise Ships

So how did I get the cruise ship gig?

I was shamed into auditioning, that's how.

It was 1992, I was deep into the broke actor thing in L.A. I worked for a messenger service in Burbank during the day and did theater in Orange county at night. For those of you who don't have a working knowledge of the geography of Southern California, Burbank is just north of downtown L.A. & Orange county, where I was performing, is about 40 miles south. I was actually living in the back room of the messenger service (I said BROKE actor, right?) I would get up at 5AM, start deliveries to the movie studios around 5:30, work til mid-afternoon, drive down to the O.C., sleep in my car for an hour or two, perform in a show, then drive back to Burbank by midnight-ish and start again the next morning. By Thursday or Friday the sleep deprivation would start to kick in. I was once woken up while driving back home after a show by a policeman's spot shining in my face. On the 5 Freeway. While driving. Yeah, I know…

While broke, I was still finding the money to study with a great vocal coach in Studio City named Lee Sweetland. Lee and his wife Sally, who was also his accompanist, had a studio that included a lot of celebrities, but they also liked working with struggling artists, hence my inclusion. The student right after me was a fairly well known actress named Chelsea Fields, who once told me I had a beautiful voice. I was kinda transfixed, but she had just gotten out her Mercedes and I was about to get into my old Ford Focus, so I just thanked her and moved along.

Lee knew that I was preparing for an audition for Norwegian Cruise lines, or Jean Ann Ryan Productions, who ran the entertainment for NCL back then. I actually had a lesson with Lee right before the audition, which was at Debbie Reynolds studios in North Hollywood. But that morning I woke up with the beginnings of a cold. Congestion, sinus headache, all of the above. I went to the lesson with Lee, because I had already paid and in those days you didn't miss just because you didn't feel 100%.

But when I got to the lesson I told Lee " I'm not going to go to the audition. I don't want to go there when I'm not at my best. It seems like a waste of time".

Lee's response?

"Oh, so that's your excuse? You don't feel perfect? So what's it going to be next time, hmm?. Why are you even studying if you're not serious about working? Is this just a hobby? That's why you moved to California and worked so hard? To find a reason to not actually audition when it's time? Sally and I have both worked when we weren't 100% (Sally agreed here). We thought you were serious about this".

53

You get the idea.

I told him "I'm not dressed for the audition and I didn't bring my stuff".

"Well, what do you have?"

"Umm, an old resume, no headshot and the music I brought for us to work on".

"Do you have time to go back home?"

"No".

"Then I guess that's what you're going with".

That wasn't a question. So, I did. I went straight to Debbie Reynolds. With half a voice, in whatever clothes I had on, with an old resume and no headshot. I sang "If Ever I would Leave You" because the cold had taken away my high notes and it's a low song. I walked out of there thinking "Well, that was a waste of time but at least I can tell Lee & Sally that I did it."

2 weeks later I got a call from Jean Ann Ryan productions asking whether I was available to travel to Ft. Lauderdale, start rehearsals and bring out a brand new cruise ship, NCL's Windward, for a 15 month contract. To someone who was living in the back room of a messenger service in Burbank, the idea of living on a cruise ship in the Caribbean and singing for a living sounded, well, pretty damn good. But it was because Lee & Sally had enough faith in me to push me harder than I pushed myself. I thank them for the faith and for the push.

And that's how I ended up working on ships for 4 years.

12-Missing the Boat

"Sea Legs" Circus, M/S Windward . And yes, that's the late, great Kurt Thomas.

When you work on cruise ships, there are a few rules.

- Don't hook up with the passengers.

- If you do hook up with a passenger, make sure it's not a passenger that an officer is interested in hooking up with.

- Don't bring drugs on or off the ship, unless the idea of being tried and imprisoned in a foreign country is a life experience you just have to sample.

- Don't miss the ship.

This last one seems like the easiest, and is true for guests and employees alike. If you miss the ship as a passenger, you get to transport yourself to the next port, or to the home port, where you wait until all the passengers who didn't miss the boat disembark, then you get to come back onboard, pack up your stuff and go home. If you're an employee, you also get to transport yourself to the next port, plus you may get fired, get fined, get confined to quarters, etc.

But it's pretty simple, right? Don't miss the ship. Well...I had been on the ship for about a year. We had rehearsed 3 new shows in Florida, flown to France and brought the brand new M/S Windward across the Atlantic. We had done a summer of cruising in the Caribbean and were traveling through the Panama canal and up the west coast to spend the summer cruising the inside passage of Alaska. During this time, in addition to performing in the shows, I had taken on the role of "Crew Bar & Store Manager".

That sounds way more impressive than it is. The crew bar and the crew store are both just what they sound like. A place on board for the crew, who work crazy long hours, many 7 days a week, to relax or pick up needed sundry supplies. The drinks in the bar were cheap, and the supplies were priced low as well. And no, you as a passenger can't go there...

...Though years later, as a passenger, I did. I faked my way into a crew bar to watch the UEFA soccer final between Bayern Munich & my team, Chelsea. They weren't showing it in passenger areas, so I casually asked my room steward where the crew bar was, he gave me a general idea, and I faked my way in. One thing about a ship's crew is that people come and go, so a new face doesn't exactly stick out. But when I got to the bar, I was reminded that a lot of the officers on the ship were German, and therefore fans of Bayern Munich, because there they were, all avidly waiting for the match to begin. What did I do? Acted like I belonged there, walked up to the bar and ordered a drink.

I made it to halftime. I didn't get busted, but I got enough side eyes from people that my "spider-senses"were screaming at me to leave, so I made my way back to the passenger area. And BTW, Chelsea won in a huge upset.

…but I digress.

So I was the manager of the crew bar & store. There was actually a guy who's job was to bartend in the bar and clerk the store. He did all the work. But I was basically the liaison between him and the officers. I would rubber stamp his work and deal with any issues that he needed help with. And no, I did not make any money for this. Strictly pro bono. I dug the fact that I got to interact with most of the crew as something more than a performer. Performers were resented by some crew members because we only "worked" 3 days a week. It was a very cushy gig, by ship standards. In this role, I knew most of the officers. And they knew me. In fact I had just broken up a fight between 2 drunk officers WAY after hours in the bar.

One of the stops on our "repositioning cruise" was Los Angeles. I hadn't been back to L.A. since I got the job , and I had plans while we were in town. I wanted to visit my old boss in Burbank, say hello to some friends in Orange County, grab some L.A. food I was missing, and get back to the ship in Long Beach.

A word about L.A. traffic.

I know that you know it's bad. And that's true, it is bad, even at the best of times. But one of the things about L.A. traffic is it can be bad at any time, day or night. I once got done with a video shoot at 1:30am and got caught in a traffic jam on the 101. At 2:00 in the morning. There is no rhyme or reason to L.A. traffic.

So, I was fine until I got to Orange county. I had 90 mins to get back to the ship. Should have been enough time to get there, return the rental car and board the ship. But, and my apologies if you don't know L.A. freeways, the 22 freeway was a parking lot. I started to break out in a cold sweat. I start asking God for favors. Evidently God had better things to do. By the time I get to Long Beach and drop the rental car, it's 10 mins past the last boarding and the ship should be departing like, now. I run the few blocks from the rental return to the onboarding and see the ship, about 100 yards off the dock and heading to San Fransisco. So. What now?

I'll have to find a flight out of Long Beach or Orange county to San Fransisco. It's gonna cost an arm and a leg. But that's about my only choice. What else can I do?

"Hey, you on that ship?" One of the dock crew.

"Umm, I'm supposed to be."

"What happened?" No, really. He asked that.

I'm not making excuses. "I missed it. That's what happened"

"What's your name"

"Robert Tully"

He talks into a walkie. "Stick around."

And...the ship comes back & puts down a gangway.

I get on and the security guy says "Staff Captain's office. Now" So that's where I go. He's waiting for me there. He still has a bit of the black eye that he got in the fight. He asks for an explanation. I tell him what happened.

"Go to your cabin. As far as anyone else is concerned, you're confined to your quarters when you're not needed for shows".

"As far as anyone else is concerned..?"

"Shut up. Get out of my office".

Lesson? I don't know. Something about not trusting L.A. traffic? Something about pro bono work and fringe benefits..? You decide. But in the great big world of people, I'm pretty sure I'm in a small minority of folks who have had a cruise ship pull back into a port to pick them up.

So I've got that going for me.

Which is nice.

13-Lightning

I'm back in Cincinnati. It's 1994.

I've just finished 15 months at sea with Norwegian cruise lines and flown back to visit Mom, family, etc. The plan was to buy a car, drive back to L.A. and start rehearsals for a show. So I spent some time with family & friends and bought a car. A Ford Fiesta, to be exact. Used, to be sure. Cheap, to be honest. But, transportation. Wheels to get me to L.A. and get me around while I was there. I knew I was going back to ships after the show, but you can't really exist in L.A. for 3 months without a car, so it filled the bill.

I took some time to make up a bit of an itinerary. How far I was going each day, what hotels I was going to stay at, that sort of thing. It gave me a basic idea of how far I wanted to get each day and where I was staying. Nice, but affordable hotels. More importantly, it gave my Mom a feeling of comfort, knowing where I was, that I was safe, etc.

Because Eileen worried. Even after I had left town for California, lived as a broke actor, worked on a cruise ship as a performer, etc. Eileen still worried. It's probably a Mom thing, but it was definitely my Mom's thing. More about Eileen in another blog. In fact, she gets her own. But she did take comfort in knowing where I was going to be during my trip. And I had what I called a "Mom" policy. Mom had helped me out in the past. a little cash here & there. But at one point I decided that if I was going to take this alternative route with my life, I should have to foot the bill for it. So she didn't hear about the really tough, "sleeping in the back office of the messenger service" times. She didn't need that. She had done enough and more for her 5 kids. She didn't need to worry about the challenges that her late 20-ish son faced because he decided to go to L.A. with aspirations and a girl. This way, she had my itinerary for this trip and that gave her comfort. So I said my goodbyes, Mom cried, as she always did when any of her children left, and off I went.

Day1- Cincinnati to Memphis. It's about 475 miles, a 7 or 8 hour drive. I've got a Motel 6 picked out to stay in. It's a easy days drive but a good start. And the day goes smoothly. This is the 2nd time I've driven from Cincinnati to L.A., the 1st time being when I loaded up my Cutlass Supreme in 1987 to join my girl in Modesto to start my California adventure. So I was comfortable with the idea of driving across the country.

I got to Memphis around 4:00-4:30 pm. Like I said, it was an easy, smooth drive. I wasn't tired, so I referred to my AAA triptik. (yes, this was before an app on your smartphone did everything but drive for you) and saw that Little Rock, Ark was a scant 150 miles further. 2 1/2 more hours off of my trip? Why not?

So off I went to Little Rock. The trip started off well enough, but there were storm clouds on the horizon. That sounds like a metaphor. But no, there were literally storm clouds. On the horizon. Big, ominous looking storm clouds. And I swear to you this is true. You won't believe me of course. You'll think it's me imagining things after the fact.

But I was scared.

As the storm clouds approached and the rain started, sprinkles first and then gradually harder, and thunder rolled and lightning flashed, I was truly afraid. I scoffed at my own fear;

"My God, have you been away from the Midwest so long that you're scared of a little rain and thunder ?

"No."

"Then what's up?"

"Nothing. Shut up."

And so on. Me, myself & I having a little convo. And in the midst of said convo...

"BLAM!!!!!!"

A crazy loud peal of thunder. I hadn't even seen the lightning. At least it didn't register with me. But all of the sudden, my car just shut off. I was going 75-80 miles an hour and suddenly 2 of my tires were flat and the engine shut off. I somehow muscled the car over to the side of the road, more out of instinct than anything else, before the momentum gave out.

Stranded. On the side of the road. Car won't start. 2 flat tires.

Well, first I sat there and tried to figure out what had just happened. One second; 4 good tires, 1 good engine, 75 mph. Next second; 2 blown tires, 1 dead engine, 0 mph. 1 large BLAM!!

Is this even possible? Could my car have been struck by lightning? I've never heard of such a thing. And again, I can't just pull my phone out and look up "lightning strikes car". Much less call for help. I'd have to find one of those roadside call boxes. Had I seen one? Nope. Who looks for those when you're tooling along, carefree, to your next destination?

Stuck. Stranded. S.O.L.

But then a car pulls up behind me. A local good Samaritan and there is no sarcasm in that statement. Even the most sarcastic people can recognize and appreciate help when it's needed. We get out of our cars.

"Thanks for stopping"

"You're welcome. What seems to be the problem?"

"Well, I'm not sure what happened, but I think my car got struck by lightning"

Beat…..beat…"uh-huh"..

So I explain what happened. He still doesn't really believe me, but he tells me that he'll call the local tow company there in Hazen, Ark.

Yup. Hazen. 90 miles outside of Little Rock.

I thank him, he wishes me well, gets in his car and drives off. About an hour later a tow truck drives up, and we have the same conversation.

"Thanks for coming"

"What the problem?"

" I think my car got struck by lightning"

"…uh-huh".

But then he looks the car over and says. "I've never heard of it, but with the tires and all, it makes as much sense as anything. I'm going drop you at a local hotel and tomorrow we can figure out what to do."

So I stay the night at a quaint little hotel in Hazen. The next morning we figure out that the nearest repair shop that can deal with, well, whatever has happened to my car is actually a Ford dealership in Little Rock. So, a 90 mile tow to the dealer. When I get there, I have a 3rd version of the same conversation, except this time with an after- exam add-on;

"Umm Mr. Tully, we examined your vehicle and it seems that your car was stuck by lightning"

Thanks for that.

"It went in via the antenna, through the engine and out through the tires. If you had been touching the ground during all this…?"

" Yeah that crossed my mind…"

"Well, luckily you weren't. As it is, we are going to have to replace most all of the electrical components of your car. As well as the tires."

The good news was that it was 1994. And I was driving an '88 Ford Fiesta. "Most of the electrical" on a 88 Fiesta didn't amount to all that much. But between the tow and the repair, my cruise gig nest-egg was a lot smaller than I planned. However, I covered the bill, spent 1 more day in beautiful Little Rock and then was on my way. Lighter in the wallet but still moving, praise Allah.

Now, about Eileen.

I told Mom I would call every night. And she had an itinerary, listing where I would be and when I would be there. So that's what she got.

-The night I spent in Hazen, she got a call telling her I was safe & sound in Memphis.

-The next night, waiting for my car in Little Rock. I called to let her know that I was in Oklahoma City. It was a beautiful place and the drive had been scenic.

-The next day I called from OK City, letting her know that Albuquerque was very nice and I'd be getting L.A. the next day.

And so on.....

She found out the truth about a month later. I was safe & sound, the show was up & running, and enough time had passed that she could, eventually, see the humor. Of course she scolded me and told me to "never do that again". I laughed and told her that I wouldn't. I knew that I would, and, bless her heart, so did she.

And I did.

But those are other stories.

14-The Circus

The Hanging   The Circus

The first question people ask, after making the requisite joke about running away with the circus, is "How did you get that job?"

It was 1997. I'd just gotten back from 4 years with Norwegian Cruise Lines where, ironically enough, I was the Ringmaster of a circus themed cruise ship show for the better part of 4 years. (Oh the foreshadowing) I was back working at Knotts Berry Farm and doing the occasional local theater gig. I had actually just been cast as "the Executioner" in a Knotts Scary Farm show called "The Hanging". Knotts was one of the first parks to really embrace the Halloween scare concept and they actually did it really well. I was kinda happy to get that gig, because I could work during the day at my regular park gig, playing "Dakota Dan" in their Calico Saloon show, then come back in the evening for the Scary Farm gig. "The Hanging" was an outdoor stunt show and the Executioner was the emcee of it. So I had that going on at the time when I saw an audition notice in Dramalogue, a casting paper back in the day. And yes, it was a "paper". You had to wait until it came out on Thursdays and find a store that carried it. You kids and your internet driven instant gratification, don't get me started.

The audition notice read "Come to the Anaheim Pond and audition to become the Ringmaster of the Greatest Show on Earth".

And, btw, it's "Ringmaster". If I had a dime for every time someone asked me what it was like to be a "ringleader"… No, I didn't start a coup in a small South American country. I was the Master of Ceremonies for the circus…

…but I digress.

So I read this, saw it was on a Tuesday, looked at my schedule, saw the I was free on Tuesday and thought "What else am I doing?" And the Pond was the arena where the Mighty Ducks played (it's the Honda Center now). The audition said bring a song so I thought "Cool! I get to sing at in an arena!"

Did I really think I would get cast as the Ringmaster of RBB&B? Heck no. When I was a kid we had gone to the Cincinnati Gardens to see the RBB&B circus, staring Gunther Goebel Williams.

Me, be the Ringmaster of that show? C'mon now.

What I was going to do was sing & do whatever else they wanted me to do until they cut me. It would be a fun day. So I get there on the day. There are about 100-150 other people there to audition. We're on one side of the arena. There's a group of people sitting on the other side, which I subsequently found out were the circus performers.And there were camera crews from several local TV stations. One thing I would learn was that with Ringling, EVERYTHING was a P.R. opportunity. P.T. Barnum's spirit was alive and well.

So I sit back and wait until they call my name. I get up and sing a bit of "This is the Moment". The money notes at the end. If you know, you know. Ok, not bad. Not great, but not bad. And I wait. They get through everyone and then announce the names of about 20 people who should stay. And lo & behold, my name's called. Cool. I'm still not thinking about getting the job but hey, let's hang around.

Next we do some announcing. "Ladies and gentlemen, children of all ages". That sort of thing. And then they cut again. Again, I hear my name. OK, now this is getting interesting. There's about 10 of us now.

Next up, we do some improv with one of the stars of the show, a clown named David L. OK, it feels alright, I don't think I got an "A" but I passed. They call 6 names, mine included, and ask us to come down to talk. The message to us was " That's all we're doing today. We'll make our decision in the next couple weeks and let you know either way.

Now I still didn't really think I was going to get the gig. You see , there was a guy named Steven there. I knew Steven because of the production of 1776 at Long Beach Civic Light Opera, which we've already talked about. The one that starred Dean Jones and a list of other name actors. Steven played a major role and I played the smallest role in the show. Steven had major credits and was obviously the best thing in the room at the RBB&B auditions. All you needed was 2 eyes, 2 ears and a brain to know that. So I walked away happy that I had done good work and gotten as far as I did.

Fast forward 3 weeks.

It's October and I am deep into Halloween season at Knotts. The Scary Farm is a big money maker so we are doing as many shows as they can cram into the schedule. Doing the day shows, doing the night shows. Thrashing my voice, but making what was , for me at the time, bank. One day my phone rings and it's the casting guy for Ringling.

Several mistakes happen at this point.

He tells me that they would like me to be the Ringmaster for the 127th edition of Ringling Bros. & Barnum and Bailey circus, Red unit, for 1998. Am I available?

I say "Yes".

This was not one of the mistakes.

They congratulate me, then get down to business. "We should discuss salary. Just so you know, you were not our first choice"

"Yeah, what happened with Steven?"

" How do you know we offered it to Steven?"

"Because I have 2 eyes, 2 ears and a brain" (as I shared with you earlier)

"Yes, we couldn't agree on details about money, etc."

"OK"

"So what would you consider a fair salary for this role?"

Here comes mistake #1 Never. Let me repeat. NEVER go into salary negotiations without researching the job. In fact, as an actor, here is one of those moments when your agent makes his 10%. Unless, of course, you don't have an agent. Which I didn't. Nor did I do any research on the role, money, etc. All I had was my previous experience in paying jobs. At that point, the best gig I had ever booked, money-wise, was as a singer for Norwegian cruise lines.

So what would have been the smart move?

Not answering the question. That would have been the move to make. Let them make an offer and go from there. Tell them you'll get back to them and go ask some people who might know. That would have made sense.

Did I do either of those things? Nope. What I did was, I took the best money I had made with NCL, added a few hundred to it, and led with that.

Now. Here's when I realized that I had screwed up. When, in negotiating a salary, you name a number and their counter offer is $400 HIGHER than your opening gambit? You know you have well and truly screwed up. I actually admire the fact that he didn't laugh out loud on the phone, but I've got to think there was a little humor had at my expense after the call was over.

That was mistake #1 On to mistake numero dos.

They ask how soon I can join them to train with the current Ringmaster. I tell them that I'm obligated to finish the Halloween contract with Knotts and we close on the 1st of November. They say "Great. We'll fly you to Chicago on Nov. 2 and get started." And I agree. Did you see the part above where I said that I was working my butt off at Knotts and my voice was thrashed? So, no rest. No time to get healthy and make a good first impression. Nope. None of that.

They send me the vocal tracks, so I can practice. There are 6 songs and you're working with a 7 piece live band , which is very cool. What was not cool was my predecessor in the role is a marvelous tenor, whom they have written the songs for. I'm a baritone. I let them know that there's no way I can sing these songs in the current key. Their response was "Oh, we'll work that out when you get here". So I just work on memorizing and have faith that, being professionals, they know what they are doing.

So I close "The Hanging" and fly to Chicago on the evening of the 2nd. The next morning, the first thing they have me do is sing through the songs with the band in the arena. This is their idea of "working it out when I get here". Having me sing the songs in the original key in front of God & everyone. Most of the circus people are there. Also there is the guy who owns the circus. And Disney on Ice. And touring shows and Broadway shows. Kenneth. I'm told later that he usually has a hand in selecting Ringmasters. They are actually a big thing in the circus world. And he's here to see who they have selected in his absence. That would be me. Singing songs that are in a tenor key. With a thrashed voice.

It was ugly. I knew it would be as soon as I realized what the setup was. It was kind of like a comedian dying. In front of a crowd that he was going to work, travel & live with. They didn't know the back story. All they knew was what they heard. And that wasn't pretty. At all.

Oh well. You get over things.

We worked out the keys. I learned to do the crazy number of shows that we did in that year. When I met Gunther Goebel Williams, who was still with the circus, though his son Mark Oliver was actually doing the act. As a greeting, all he said to me was;

"You need to be here. All the time. I am here all the time. You must be here."

Then he turned and walked away. Not "Welcome". Not "Glad to have you". Just that.

So I did what he asked. We did 10, 11, 12 show weeks, traveled all over the country, plus Mexico, which is a separate story. I got tired. Early on I overworked my voice. I got sick. But I never missed a show. It wasn't always pretty. But that's one thing I can say about that year. Every time they rang the bell I got up off the stool.

Oh, and Kenneth and I? Nope. In this scenario, I think of myself as Dan Driessen.

Who was Dan Driessen, you ask? Dan Driessen was the 1st baseman for the Cincinnati Reds who replaced Tony Perez. Tony Perez was a beloved player who was part of the Big Red Machine. Pete Rose, Johnny Bench, Joe Morgan, all of the stars that old school Cincinnati Reds fans remember better than the current Reds lineup. And Dan? Dan was the next guy. He was the guy who replaced Tony Perez when Tony left the Reds. Dan Driessen was a good player. He did a good job. But he wasn't Tony Perez.

My predecessor was Ringmaster for 11 years. He was an amazing singer and Kenneth loved him. And I was Dan Driessen. We got through the year. But that ice never thawed. And there was never a question about me doing a 2nd contract.

But that's how I got the job as Ringmaster for Ringling Bros. & Barnum and Bailey circus.

Thanks for asking.

15-A quick word about Tigers & Trainers

Never turn your back on a tiger. Or trust a German animal trainer.

During my year with Ringling Bros., one of our early stops was Little Rock, Arkansas. We were mid-performance and I was standing near the tiger cage, waiting for the high wire act to finish so I could "out-tro" them and intro the tiger act. When the Guerrero family finished on the high wire, I would jump up on a bull tub (the big round things which dot the circus floor) the spot light would hit me, and I'd start talking. While I waited, I was chatting with star of the tiger act, Gunther's son Mark. I'm facing Mark with my back to the tiger cage & I've got one eye on the high wire, when Mark takes a casual step or two to the side and sort of indicates to the cage behind me. So I turn to see what he's looking at. What I see is, maybe 5 feet away from me, in the cage, the back end of a tiger. With his tail up.

When you were a kid, on a hot summer day, did you ever play around with the garden hose, maybe stick your thumb in the hose and spray each other? Well, if you turned the water way up, that was what happened to me. Except it wasn't water. And it wasn't cool. I was literally hosed down with tiger pee. Sprayed from head to toe. Then the high wire act ended and I got hit with a spotlight. In front of 20,000-ish paying customers.

As I stood on the bull tub, covered in tiger pee, doing the out-tros and intros, all the circus folks were convulsed with laughter. The audience didn't know, because I was in the dark when I got sprayed. But my co-workers were totally in on it. I didn't find it nearly as funny as they did, but I'm a professional, so I stood there for about a minute and a half, doing my thing in a soggy ringmaster outfit. When I was done and the spotlight was off me, I had some choice words for any and all as I ran back to change into a fresh outfit, but the circus isn't a place for the weak or meek, so I took it in stride as part of the initiation in the their world. In retrospect, it was maybe the most honest welcome I got to the world of circus.

But I swear that tiger looked at me differently for the rest of the year.

I'll leave it there.

16-Mexico City

When they hired me as Ringmaster, the good folks at Ringling told me that the circus would play Mexico City for 2 weeks in June and that I would need to learn the show in Spanish. I told them I didn't speak Spanish but if they got me the script immediately after we opened, I would study it phonetically. Which is what I did, though I had to raise hell with them to finally get the Spanish script, a month **after** we opened.

But I took the script and studied it, day after day, week after week, until about a month before we were to travel to Mexico. At that point the bosses let me know that they had actually hired an actor who starred in a Mexican telenovela to be the Ringmaster in Mexico City.

Super. Thanks.

As it turned out, Roberto Miguel and I became good friends. First off, my first and middle names are "Robert Michael", so he and I had pretty much the same name. And he was a genuinely great guy, so we got along very well. During the shows at the Palacio Deportes in Mexico City, Roberto would perform the role of Ringmaster, and I would guide him from place to place so he wouldn't get run over or smashed by any of the set pieces or animals moving around in the dark.

I played my role, guiding Roberto around. And, because I had studied the script for so long, I would mouth the words as he said them. I even got to deliver some lines during Roberto's rehearsals. So he knew that I knew the Spanish. Which is why I doubt the official version of what happened next.

About a week into performances, I got a call in the afternoon. It seemed that Roberto had come down with a case of food poisoning, so if possible I would be needed to actually do the show that night. In Spanish. Which is what I did. At the Palacio Deportes. In front of a crowd of around 20,000

Folks, it was the scariest thing I have ever done. Scarier that bungie jumping in Africa (we'll discuss this later), scarier than getting beat up in New Orleans.(again, later). My knees were literally shaking during the opening number, though luckily the audience can't see my legs because I'm riding on a float at that point.

How did it go? The floor crew, who do all of the real work setting up, tearing down and making the in-show changes, came up to me afterwards and said "We didn't know you spoke Spanish!" I count that as a win.

Now. Did Roberto, who knew I had taken the time to learn the show in Spanish, and was a native of Mexico City, really get food poisoning? Possibly. But that's not the bet I would make, if I had to put money on it. The next day, Roberto was recovered. In fact, he didn't seem at all the worse for wear.

I guess that's how it is with food poisoning.

I guess.

17-D.C. running

My year with the circus was when my running went from an occasional alternative to my gym workouts and became a passion of its own. Because I was touring the country on a train, I didn't have regular access to a gym, so running was something I could do no matter what train yard we were stopped in. The first race I ever ran was when we were in Dallas . A 5k called the "Clowns & Clones 5k" . Don't ask me why Clowns & Clones, or whether the clowns had anything to do with the circus (they didn't) or what kind of clones. I don't recall. But it seemed like a logical next step, and it started me down this road that has taken me literally all over the world.

But that's not the story I'm telling here.

We're in Washington D.C., playing several different venues in the area. The train is parked in a train yard (duh) and I decide to go for a run. Remember, this is 1998. Not pre-cell phone but pre- cell phone with all the bells and whistles that we take for granted today. So you can't just open Maps on your iPhone to find your way.

In those days, when going for a run in an unfamiliar city, the rule was to limit your twists and turns. Try to straight line it so that you can simply turn around and head back . At least as much as possible. So I head out for a 3 or 4 mile run. Maybe 40 mins or so. I get about 20 mins in and what do I see in the distance?

The Capitol Dome.

Hey, wouldn't it be cool to run up the steps of the Capitol Dome? Damn right it would be. So off I go. Easy enough. Just keep the dome in sight and keep angling towards it. Is this going to be a little longer than my 3-4 miles? Sure. But hey, life experience, man.

So I get there. To the Capitol. Now I'm going to go "Rocky"style up the steps, maybe do a little dance at the top, and head home. That's until I see the guys at the top of the steps. In sunglasses & suits. With conspicuous bulges where, say, guns would be. So, OK, no Rocky moment at the top. I run about half way up, turn around a just head home.

You see my mistake here, right?

Getting there, I always had the Dome to aim for. There's no Capitol dome at the train yard. There's no dome at all. Or anything else that would act as a beacon. But I'm not really worried. I have this unreasonable, and as it turns out, unrealistic, confidence in my ability to find my way back. So I head out in the direction of the train yard, as far as I know.

Turn follows turn. Turn turns into turned around. Confidence gives way to uncertainty. It's been an hour and a half. Where am I? Where is the train yard? Lots of questions. Not many answers.

Another thing about D.C. is that it is our nation's Capitol. But it also contains some, well, rather dicey neighborhoods. And guess where the train yard lies. Yup. Smack dab in the middle of it all. As train yards tend to. So, I haven't found the train yard, but I have certainly found the neighborhood. And it's late afternoon, the suns going down and in this particular part of the world, there aren't a lot of other folks out for a jog.

Hmm.

So I'm just keeping myself to myself, hoping to see something, anything that would give me a clue. And now I'm aware that a car has slowed down and is pacing me. I haven't looked, but I feel it. Oh crap. Just keep your head down, keep moving, maybe they'll just go away. Maybe it's nothing. Then, a voice.

"Hey!"

Just keep running.

"Hey, you lost?"

I turn and look. It's the cops.

" Uh yeah. Lost."

"Where are you trying to get to?"

"The train yard"

"Why the train yard?"

"I'm with the circus. Can you give me directions?"

"Nope. Get in. You're in the wrong neighborhood my friend".

So, I get in. On the way to the yard, which is only about 2 blocks away, the one cops tells me that he was hoping to get to the circus this weekend. With his wife. And his 2 kids.

Best seats in the house. You betcha.

18-The Faith

And by the faith I mean Catholicism. Or, in my neighborhood when I was growing up, the only game in town. In Cincinnati, especially on the west side in the 60s & 70s, every neighborhood had 3 things. A bar, a chili parlor and a Catholic church. We kids were raised Catholic. At St.William's elementary school and, in my case, Archbishop Elder high school. My older sister went to St. Elizabeth Seton H.S., the girls Catholic school, which was located about 100 yards from Elder. My 3 younger siblings opted for Western Hills H.S., the public high school in the area.

And I did the whole 9 yards. I sang in the church choir and was a server at Mass. I even considered the priesthood for a short time during my high school years. That was before I discovered women. After that happened, the priesthood lost a lot of it's luster in my estimation. But I was connected to the church until my late 20's, mostly through music. I sang in the adult choir at St. Williams after I graduated from Elder, and sang in their show choir, the St. Williams Singers. And most of my social circle were church related as well.

I am not currently a practicing Catholic. Travel and lifestyle took me away from the church. And, to be honest, I never really bought the whole transubstantiation thing. When the priest would say "the body of Christ" I would reply with the required "Amen", but it was more rote than belief. And it was the same with most of the sacraments. So around my late 20's, when I left for California, I said goodbye to active participation in the faith. I would attend mass when it was a part of the social agenda, like a friend getting married, a kid's first communion, or whenever I was home and Mom wanted to go. Yeah, I never saw the harm in going along. I wasn't enough of a hypocrite to take communion, but I would attend.

And though I am no longer am a practicing Catholic, I am glad I was raised in the faith. I do think there is a great deal of value in organized religion. I think that Catholicism gave me a set of rules growing up. A basic guideline for behaving and treating my fellow man. And an example of the difference that charity can make in the world. And coming back to Cincinnati and being exposed to those communities has shown me the social value of the church. It gives many people a place to go, a schedule of activities to be involved in, a peer group. I have met people I went to grade school with who are still close to folks from our graduating class. That shocked me a bit, as I'm not really sure I could name more than a dozen, much less connect with them. But I think that it's a cool thing.

Am I aware of the scandals connected with the Catholic church? Of course. Priests who taught me in school have been implicated. So yeah, I know that things happened, and were covered up. I am also a member of the performing arts community and spent 20 years in the business world. That kind of reprehensible behavior occurs everywhere. I think it's the people, not the institution. In my time in L.A., I was offered a role in a show in exchange for sexual favors, straight up and bluntly. When I was looking for an apartment, I was offered one monthly rate and a second, lower rate, if I allowed the landlord to occasionally "spend the night".

Just FYI, I politely declined his offer. At either rate....

...but I digress.

So I credit the faith with giving me a lot. Values, social interaction and friendships. I respect my friends who are still active in the faith. To me, it doesn't make sense to use logic to discredit someone else's religious beliefs. It's right there in the word.

Faith.

They have faith. Faith transcends logic and cold hard facts. If it makes you happy and doesn't hurt others, why not?

Again.

What makes you happy and doesn't hurt others.

Amen.

19-Huis Ten Bosch

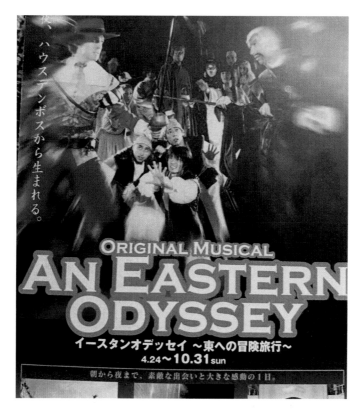

Yup. The bad guy. Again.

How did Japan and Huis Ten Bosch happen? Another audition notice in Backstage. Another visit to an audition venue in North Hollywood. Another callback and interview. By late 2003 I had been back in L.A. since the end of my Ringling Bros. gig. About 4 years of Knotts Berry Farm during the day, Curtain Call theater at nights. Basically, broke actor days again.

The Knotts gig was semi-regular. I had guaranteed hours and benefits, but I wasn't getting rich. In fact I was slowly getting poor. I was pretty regularly behind on rent & car payments, and knew the guy at the "payday loans" place on a first name basis.

So when the audition, callback & interview went well, and the folks at Huis Ten Bosch offered me a job, I jumped at it. Much like ships, it was what they paid me plus what I didn't have to pay for (rent, food, transportation, etc.)

Now I know what your next question is. What's a Huis Ten Bosch? Well, if you knew Dutch you wouldn't be asking that question. But for the rest of you, Huis Ten Bosch means "House in the Woods". It is an amusement park which replicates the city of Amsterdam. On the Japanese island of Kyushu. Huis Ten Bosch is about 50 miles north of Nagasaki. And by replicates Amsterdam, I mean when it was built, they imported the bricks from Europe to build the buildings and walkways and bridges over the canal. There are canal cruisers, just like you'd see in Amsterdam. Fields of tulips. Tall sailing ships. The whole 9 yards.

All this was done long before I was hired, and it had posed several problems throughout the history of the park. First of all, as I mentioned above, the park is north of Nagasaki and far from Fukuoka, the largest city on Kyushu. If you know your Japanese amusement parks, you know that Disney Japan is located near Tokyo. Universal Japan is near Osaka. Both large cities with numerous other tourist attractions and reasons to visit. The nearest city to Huis Ten Bosch is Sasebo. There is a U.S. Naval base there. That's about it. Lovely city, but not really a reason to jump on a plane and spend tourist dollars. Also, Disney and Universal are globally recognized brands, with numerous other locations.

Have you heard of Huis Ten Bosch?

That's what I thought. It's the one and only .

As a result of these and other factors, Huis Ten Bosch had been in & out of bankruptcy several times in its history. Their idea of an entertainment program was hiring random acts and placing them in locations around the park. But in 2003 the park was taken over by new ownership and the plan was to create a "Disney-like" entertainment program. The park management hired an American production company, who then planned, created and cast the entire park's entertainment. There were 30-40 Japanese performers and about the same number of non-Japanese, mostly U.S. based performers. of which I was one.

My performance day was;

-AM. Play the comic villain in the "Good Day Show".

-Do several tours in close harmony quartets and octets.

-PM.Sing with a 12 piece big band, along with other vocalists.

-Play the bad guy villain in the "Eastern Odyssey" action/stunt show.

It had the opportunity to be a fun, challenging, entertaining experience. However…

There were several challenges. The first and probably most serious issue was that the American production company wasn't actually a production company. It was the creation of someone who had worked as a dancer and a casting agent in L.A., and had sold the Japanese producers on his ability to create, cast and deliver the product. For an outrageous amount of money. He knew dance and choreography, but not so much about music and acting. And he was our director. I once sat and listened to him tell the company about the importance of observing "the 3rd wall" in acting. Mentioned it several times in his talk. I actually looked around for anyone else who might have heard and understood the irony. Either no one else did or they were much better at hiding their feelings.

Also, either there was no Musical Director present at the auditions, or they didn't know that we were going to be singing close harmony at the park, because part singing, especially close harmony without accompaniment, is a whole different skill than solo singing. The result of that was that about half of the people hired to do the job were not equipped to. And if 2 of your 4 singers, or 3 of your 8 singers, can't sing close harmony, it really doesn't matter what the others do. It's going to be bad. And it was.

Do I have perfect pitch? No. But I've sung barbershop, I've sung in a cappella groups. I have what I would call "decent relative pitch". That means I'm not perfect, but not bad. I, and others who knew what the problem was, tried to let management know.. But their answer was, "No. These people were hired to sing. There are no other jobs." So we would go out and sing. Badly.

Frustrating.

For the big stunt show, they brought in a Japanese director. He was a great part of the experience. All of the non-Japanese parts were voice-dubbed by Japanese actors, but I had learned the Japanese lines phonetically, so the director made me speak Japanese in all of the rehearsals and run-throughs. We got along. But he was blunt. After an early rehearsal he said to me, through an interpreter "I am glad they hired a real actor for this role". In front of the entire cast. The tall, blonde, leading man did not take that statement too well, which led to some amount of conflict between us. But I appreciated the compliment.

After the season, they kept some of us for a holiday program through November and December. There were rumors of a 2nd year of productions, and several of us were even rumored to be considered for management positions. But after spending so much money, getting at best mediocre product, and not seeing an increase in attendance, in 2005 they scrapped the entire program and went back to hiring individual acts.

I've always wanted to return to Huis Ten Bosch. My year in Japan taught me a lot. I loved the people, the food, the culture, basically the whole experience, with one notable exception. See next story....

20-Dentistry in Japan

This is what I would call a "legacy story". I first penned this in 2004, when I was working in Japan, long before the idea of a book ever occurred to me. I wrote this blog on MySpace. (yeah,MySpace), as it was actually happening. It amused the hell out of my mother and my uncle, back in the States.They said they felt bad but couldn't help laughing. I hope you enjoy.

More than I did.

First of all, I love Japan. I have found the people to be friendly, helpful and extremely courteous. They have helped me, both the cast members I have gotten to know and complete strangers, to make the transition to living and working in Japan. This is in no way a diatribe against them or this country.

Second, I have bad teeth. I have always had bad teeth. My family, at least on my mother's side, has always had bad teeth. And so, of course, I hate and fear the dentist. I have gone to the dentist sporadically, which has of course exacerbated the problems. I've had 2, 3 and 4 cavity days. Suffice to say that these have not been the happiest days of my life. But in the past couple of years I have been good. Thanks to the dental plan at Knotts Berry Farm, I got much of the simple cavity work and tooth cleaning done.

And so, before I left the nurturing bosom of Knotts to venture to Japan, I took one last trip to the dentist. Didn't want to, didn't enjoy it, got 2 cavities filled, but I did it. Did the right thing, guarded against the possibility of having problems in a foreign country, a stitch in time saves nine. You get the idea.

So I'm off to Japan. I'm excited and nervous about a number of things, but the one thing I don't have to worry about is dental health. Have I set it up well enough?

Tuesday, April 27th. My first day off in 3 weeks. We've just opened all the major shows. I was enjoying a bowl of won-ton soup. And while I'm enjoying this off-day treat, my tooth, the top furthest back on the right, goes sensitive. No huge deal. Like I said, I have bad teeth and this one has been occasionally prone to sensitivity. However, it doesn't go away after brushing with my favorite "sensitive teeth" toothpaste and actually gets worse, until Wednesday night I am up all night with a toothache. So there's a problem. This tooth has a filling in it already, but maybe it's something under the filling. There's only one way to find out.

I know, some of you are wincing already. But look at it from my perspective. Take a small sliver of bamboo, shove it under your fingernail and try to sleep tonight. Tomorrow morning you will be surprised how anxious you will be to do something, anything, to deal with the problem. That was me on Thursday morning.

So I call the entertainment department and tell them I have a problem. They tell me I have two problems. One, my tooth. Two, Thursday begins Japan's Golden Week.

What is Golden Week?

As best I can make out, it's the week that, for no reason that anyone has yet explained to me, everyone in Japan stops working and goes someplace else. Why? because it's a rule. In Japan, a rule is a rule. If I were to put an official looking sign by the entrance to Huis Ten Bosch that said "Give this caucasian 1000 yen", I would be rich by noon. So my problem is that all of the dentists are somewhere else. They've left, with their dentist wives and dentist children and they are staying in dentist ski resorts up north in Sapporo. However, Taramoto-san, a wondrous woman who I am convinced actually owns the park and just hires men in suits to be a figurehead, sort of like a small, Japanese Wizard of Oz, tells me that she has found a dentist who either forgot it was Golden Week or actually lives in Sapporo and had to come here for the holiday.

This dentist I will refer to as Dentist #1. They put me in a taxi (this dentist is a 20 minute ride away, in the city of Daito) with Interpreter #1, Yumiko. An additional concern of mine is that we get paid on the first of the month, so I have about 5000 yen ($50). I ask if they take Visa. Yumiko smiles and says that if there is a problem, she will take care of it. OK, fine. Now I am a foreigner who has the bad taste to get sick on Golden Week, who needs an interpreter because he can't speak the language AND can't pay his own bill.

So we get to the dentist. Yumiko pays the driver and we go in. The first thing you do in a Japanese dental office is take off your shoes and put on slippers that are approximately child's size 6. Then you shuffle over to reception, where they give you a form to fill out. Or, in this case, Yumiko fills it out after asking me all of the pertinent questions, like "do you have any sexually transmitted diseases?". And you wait.

We take x-rays, and she says it looks like there might be something under my filling.More about dentistry in Japan, they do most major work in stages. A root canal could mean 4 or 5 visits. Don't ask me why. It's a rule. So if we open up the filling and the work has to be done, I'm committing to going back to Dentist #1 in Daito as opposed to going to a dentist right next to Huis Ten Bosch, walking distance from where I'm living. Yumiko tells me they can get me into that dentist the next day and that other cast members have used him. OK, I can read the writing on the wall. They'd like me to hold off and go to the other guy. Seeing that we're ultimately spending my money, a $40 cab ride 5 or 6 times sounds a little steep. So I say "Sure, we'll wait until tomorrow. But in the meantime, could you give me something for the pain? "Ah, so, so" says the dentist, and hands me 6 pills. She tells me that she's not sure, given my size, that these will work as well for me as for a Japanese person. She doesn't say anything else on the subject, like what MIGHT help or anything, but she does express her concern.

Her concerns are nothing if not well founded. One sleepless night later, it's Friday. My appointment is at 5pm, after which the dentist (let's call him dentist #2) will be boarding a late train out to Sapporo. Earlier in the afternoon, a fellow cast member hands me some ibuprofen and says "sometimes they don't use anesthetic".

More about ibuprofen later.

I expressed my concern about paying for dentist #2 to Interpreter #1 (Yumiko) and she assured me it would be taken care of. I would be paid on Saturday, but paying for dentist #1 had almost depleted me. But as I'm being driven to dentist #2, by interpreter #2 (Jun), I feel compelled to ask whether the money thing has been dealt with. Jun looks at me in surprise and says "well, maybe they'll let you pay later". My self esteem has now left the building.

New dentist, new interpreter, same size 6 child's slippers, same x-rays, same questionnaire ("No thank you Jun. No sexually transmitted diseases, thanks for asking") This dentist gives me a shot, takes the filling out and discovers there is a need to "scrape the living pulp out". (Japanese for root canal) but this will, of course, be done in stages. He'll do the cleaning out today and put a temporary cap over medicine that he puts in the hole in my tooth. I ask, "like an antibiotic?". By the time that goes through Jun to the dentist and back, the answer is "Yes, it will be medicine."

Folks, you have to trust something. So I say "OK, it sounds good to me", and we go through the procedure. As I said, it was basically painless and I was just happy to have the hard part out of the way. So as I was getting out of the chair I ask what he can give me for the pain I will probably have in the next day or two, asI've done this sort of "root canal" thing

94

before. He says "Oh no, you may have a little pain tomorrow but none after that and what you've been taking should be fine." After we get through the process of telling me that I can pay the next time I come in, Jun and I take our leave. Jun, me and my ibuprofen.

Friends, ibuprofen is a wimp.

The pain I had in my mouth for the next two days took ibuprofen's lunch money, kicked it's butt and sent it home crying to it's ibuprofen mother. Sleep? Oh no, there was no sleep, there was laying in my bed and watching the clock tic. But the whole time, I had faith." Bob, it's a root canal. What he said notwithstanding, root canals hurt for several days. Leave it go, he's safely in Sapporo now, enjoying Golden Week. See if anyone at work has something that can help". What I got from one other performer was "You're not exceeding the recommended dosage of ibuprofen, are you?" I resisted the urge to drop him right there.

Enter our show director, Derrick. Derrick had Tylenol and lent me some. I don't care what he does for the rest of his life, I will always love him. Sunday night I was able to get some sleep. But when I woke up Monday I felt kind of odd. So I looked in the mirror and what did I see? Well, the right side of my face looked like, well, my face. Cheekbone, dimple, if that's what you call that crease coming down from my nose. You know, my face.

But the left side? Well, those of you who knew me in my larger days would have recognized the one on the left.

95

Cheekbone? nope. Crease? uncreased. Dimple? undimpled. All I needed was a couple more chins and it would have been Bob Tully circa 1985, minus the hair of course.

Pain is one thing. But looking like John Merrick, the Elephant Man, just won't do at an amusement park. I go to work, walk into Taramoto-san's office and simply look at her. She looks back at me, not comprehending for a moment. Then her eyes get very wide and she goes for an interpreter. An hour later, they tell me they have found a dentist who is in town and I would be seeing him on Tuesday . That would be today, my "off-day".

More Tylenol from Derrick, may everything he touch turn to gold, and off to bed. After work, of course. Lots of funny looks, from co-workers and visitors alike.

Today dawned bright and early. I got a phone call at 9:30 telling me to take the 10:17 train to Sasebo and meet the interpreter, Taiko (Yes, that's interpreter #3 on your scorecard) and go to the dentist (all together now, dentist #3). Caught it, got there, met interpreter #3, found the clinic, put on the child's size 6 slippers, got some new x-rays and answered the questionnaire. Again. Then the dentist took off the temporary cap with a drill and cut my gum open to swab out the infection around the tooth. How do I know he did this?

BECAUSE HE DIDN'T USE ANY f@*%ing NOVOCAINE, THAT'S WHY!!

Yes, yes I saw him coming towards me with the drill and said "umm, what's he doing?" Interpreter #3 said " He's going to take the temporary cap off to look at your tooth". I expressed my concern about putting a drill inside my fully sensitive mouth and the look I got from him was half "it'll be alright" and half "what a wimp". He said that if I feel any major pain I should raise my right hand. There were many things I wanted to say at that point. Mostly obscene. What I actually said was "Oh, OK", and bit down on my self control for several minutes. No, it wasn't horrible, but feeling someone cut into your gum was no Golden Week in Sapporo either. After we finished that little exercise, he told me that an infection had set into my gum from the cavity, but it could be dealt with antibiotics.

Antibiotics.

Hmm.

What a novel concept.

Since I had been paid on Saturday, I could pay him myself, saving myself that jab to my self esteem.

So, it's Tuesday night here in Japan. I sit, typing, doing laundry and listening to Stevie Ray Vaughn. I sit here with my swollen face and wait to see what tomorrow brings and what the bosses say. My next appointment is next Saturday with dentist #2. I know, I know, but again, you have to have faith, and at least he used novocaine.

I don't know why I felt compelled to write this rambling missive. Maybe a week of sleepless nights . Maybe I miss writing. Maybe I miss home. But if you know me you know I'd rather be here, going through all this, than be safe and bored at home.

That's the original story

It ended well. We finished the work in 2 more visits. The Japanese staff and doctors were, as always, polite, courteous and efficient. This was one of many lessons I learned during my time there.

Most of the others weren't as painful.

21-Singles Cruising

When I was finishing up my contract in Japan, back in late 2004, my thoughts turned to vacation. As in, "What would be a cool vacay after a year working in a Japanese amusement park?" As I've mentioned before, I thought I was going right back to Japan after a short break, so what would be a fun, different holiday?

Enter cruise ships.

"Why cruise ships, Bob?" I hear you asking. "Didn't you spend 4 years on ships?" And you would be right. I did spend 4 years working for Norwegian cruise lines. But that was the hook for me. I spent 4 years WORKING on ships. I wondered what it would be like to experience how the other half lives. When you work on ships, you do see all kinds of foolish behavior from folks who forget to pack their common sense, and overestimate their tolerance for UV rays and alcohol. But that's the thought that came to my mind. Let's try cruising from the passenger perspective.

Next issue. How to cruise as a single person? It's a valid question. Especially back in the 00's, people cruised as families or groups, etc. There were dinners to think of, who were you going to party, dance, connect with, etc. Especially if you're not the social butterfly type, like me. So, if I'm going to do the cruise ship thing, what are my options as a single dude?

Enter the internet. All I did was type in "singles cruising"on the search bar, hit enter, and there it was.

Singles Cruise dot com.

Actually, they are not the only singles cruise group, there are others, and in the years since I have tried other options, but when you're curious about singles cruising, Singles Cruise dot com seemed like the best place to start. What I discovered was that Singles cruise offered 8 or 10 hosted singles cruises a year. Most of the cruises sailed out of Florida. You'd book through the group and their package included the cruise plus private group parties & excusions. For this service, they would add a couple hundred bucks to your fare. There would be a pre cruise party, usually held at the designated group hotel the night before the cruise. Many of the onboard activities were focused on getting people together, with the hope of folks coupling up.

A word about that.

The 1st word is NO. These were not swingers cruises. Not necessarily. Did some of that go on? Sure. You get a group of 100, 200, or in one notable case, 600 singles together on a cruise ship and, well, things happen. There are lots of agendas….

…but I digress.

Back to 2005. So I book a cruise. Out of Miami. 7 days. Caribbean. Cool. When you get booked, you got entered into a Yahoo chat group. So people can get to know each other before the cruise.(Yes, Yahoo.This was pre Facebook, OK?) And this is where the real fun started. There was SO much, umm, well, there's really no other way to put it.

Crap-talking. Outrageous, bragadocious, obviously not in the same neighborhood as true, Crap-talking.

Pictures from the late 70's, thinly veiled references to vast wealth and even "vast-er" sexual proclivities. The "singles cruise experts" giving advice on everything from how to pack to how to dress to what parties and excursions to go on. The "young and fun" subgroup, recruiting whoever they deemed appropriate.

I was hooked. Who were these people? What kind of subculture had I stumbled into? And who could I share this with? Because folks, this was way too good to keep to myself.

Enter Mel.

Mel is a friend. Maybe my best friend. Mel is also a she. Mel and I have been through a lot together. She is a performer and we've worked together. So when I thought "who can I bring with me on this weird little trip?", Mel was my first thought.

"Hey Mel"

"Hey Bob, how's Japan?"

"Cool. Never mind that. I've booked a singles cruise out of Florida. You need to come.

"You booked a what?"

Or something like that. Anyway, Mel agreed and we got to experience, together, the Yahoo chat Singles cruise experience. And we couldn't wait. I mean Could. Not. Wait. to meet some of the people behind these posts. So we finally get to Miami, and the fun starts.

Jumping ahead a bit. I've done a number of these cruises and I think that the people fall into 3 basic categories;

1) Hook ups. These people are here to meet, and experience (wink, wink) other people. Same sex, opposite, something in between. And usually not just one. On these cruises, there exists what are known as "Trade-off Tuesdays", when the folks who hooked up on the 1st day are tired of each other and see something else shiny that catches their eye. Or "Last chance Saturday", when folks who are getting off the boat the next day decide "Oh what the hell" and make those 2am in the bar decisions. These people find each other quickly and basically get on with their business. I had a woman of a certain age (ie north of me) basically interview me in the bar of the pre cruise hotel the day before we sailed. I wasn't really giving her the answers she wanted to hear when another gentleman sat on the other side of her, gave much more, well, enthusiastic answers than I had given. They left the bar for his room about 15 mins after he sat down. Honestly, I have no problem with these folks. At least it's honest, and everyone is an adult. If that's you, cool.

2) "Social-ites".

This is where I think I fit in. You go on the cruise to get your party on, hang with people, drink, dance, all the things. If something more happens and you meet someone and things progress past the purely social stage, excellent. But you don't predicate your happiness on meeting someone. Which leads me to…

3) Looking for Love.

Ah, these folks. They come on the cruise to find someone to spend the rest of their lives with. On a cruise ship. In a group of a couple hundred people. From all over the world. And if they don't meet that special someone, and at least 95% of the time they don't, they are unhappy and disappointed. On a cruise in the Caribbean. You see them grouping up, being unhappy, complaining to the hosts because "where are all the eligible men/women?"

I also discovered that singles cruises follow a familiar pattern. Highlights include:

The pre cruise liquor run. Ships have gotten better at detecting smuggled booze, but back in the day, we would hit up a liquor store and buy enough booze to stock a good sized bar. And hide it everywhere. There were cabins that literally looked like your well-heeled friend's bar at home.

Precruise Party. Which I've already mentioned, but this is where, again, people were scoping people. Who's back, who's new, who's already paired up. That sort of thing. And where, in New Orleans, I got beat up by another singles cruiser, but that's a different story….

Dinner seating. On night one we had assigned seating. After that, we had designated singles cruise tables, but could sit wherever we wanted within those tables. This became a major source of entertainment. People would literally line up early, just so they could RUN to their favorite table as soon as the doors opened so they could save seats for their friends. The "why is he/she sitting with them ?"and "No, you can't sit here. It's saved" drama was very real and hilarious.

But back to that first cruise.

Mel and I started figuring out who was who from the Yahoo group. The biggest talkers on the group chat tended to be quiet & shy IRL. (in real life, in case you're not into the lingo) We watched the pick up lines, the drama, the dinner theatrics, the late night hook ups, the whole deal. Now, I just made that sound like we simply observed. that we were above all this.

Not quite.

Mel met a boy from Australia. He seemed nice. And sincere. It turns out he was neither. I met a girl. She actually taught the same type of cardio class I did and was based in Vegas, just a 4 hour drive for me. We had a lot in common. One thing we didn't have in common?

I was single.

Sometimes, people come on the singles cruise who are not, strictly speaking, single. And in this young ladies case, it wasn't even that she was separated or living apart. Nope. Not even close. We had a great 3-4 days on the cruise and then made plans to meet up after the cruise, in Las Vegas. We talked several times. Then, one evening, my phone rings, I answer and a male voice says;

"Who is this?"

"Umm, you called me. Who is this?"

"My name is Bill (or something like that) your number keeps coming up on my wife's phone history."

"Sir, that is something you need to discuss with your wife. But please know that you won't be seeing my number any more."

Actually, she called me back, said everything was actually just fine and that I should come up and meet her at one of the hotels. Suffice to say I did not.

So there are those stories. Here's another one.

I went on about a dozen other singles cruises, more or less. Lots of stories, but you get the idea. Mel went on another cruise, met a guy from Iowa, they kept in touch, got to know each other better and got married. He's a great guy and is a good friend of mine as well. So that can happen, too.

As I said, I probably did about 12 cruises through the years. I met great people and had great times. I've stepped away from the singles cruise thing over the last 5-6 years. I think the cruises have changed and I know I have. But they were fun, they were crazy and I've got no regrets. Except maybe the gym instructor from Vegas. And the fact that I didn't discover lip balm with SPF until my 3rd cruise.

Blistered lips can really mess with your singles cruise game.

24-The Men of Rock

Men of Rock

Paul Bradley, Jeff Hutson, Robert Tully & Kennon Wolff

Mesh shirt, pleather pants…

So , I'm back in L.A. As I mentioned in a previous piece, when I left Japan in Jan. 2005 one of my cast mates and I thought we were coming back a month later to produce shows for Huis Ten Bosch. At least that's what my cast mate told me. He spoke fluent Japanese and I did not. I'm guessing things weren't as "all set" as he made them out to be, because I never heard back from them, or him, again. I'm pretty sure he's still in Japan. He got married to a Japanese girl who performed in our shows. She was his 2nd Japanese wife. He left the 1st one in New York. But I don't know details so I can't really judge.

…But I digress.

So I'm back home in L.A. Slowly coming to the realization that I probably wasn't going back, at least not to Huis Ten Bosch. So, what to do? Well, check the casting papers, submit, etc. The working actor thing. Then a friend calls me.

"Are you going to the Men of Rock audition?"

"The what?"

"The Men of Rock audition!"

"Umm, Men of Rock?"

My friend then explains that a production company in Vegas was holding auditions for a show called, well, yeah, the Men of Rock. It was a 4 person male rock review, described as "Aerosmith meets Chippendales". It was playing at a casino and the auditions were in Vegas the following Tuesday. My question…

"You mean, like a boy band?"

"Well, I guess, kinda."

"What part of a rock singing, dancing, stripping, boy band makes you think that I would be remotely appropriate?"

"Well, I just thought I would tell you. The auditions are at the Rio Suites"

A word about the Rio Suites. Las Vegas is about a 4 hour drive from Los Angeles. Back when I was doing shows in L.A. it was a fairly common thing for us to finish a Sunday night show, drive to Vegas, stay until Tuesday morning and then drive back to L.A. for the Tuesday night show. And at that time the Rio was a nice property. Not crazy expensive, but nicer than many of the other affordable places. And even then I was all about nice hotels. So the internal discussion went something like this;

"You go to the audition. They cut you and you stay at the Rio for a day or two. Why not? What else are you doing right now?"

So, I take a look at the audition notice. I need to have a rock song to sing to and be prepared to dance. I don't sing rock, and the audition is in 4 days. So, what DO I sing, that might at least pass? I think about my karaoke songs. I do enjoy karaoke, even though I know it's not for me. I think karaoke is for people who don't have stages to sing on . But I will still get up and sing every now & again. Now, what do I sing for karaoke that might pass for rock? I decide that "She's a Lady", the Tom Jones song, is as close as I get to rock. And who cares. They are gonna cut me anyway, so let's go with that. Done deal.

So I drive up on Tuesday and head to the Rio Suites. There are probably about 30 guys waiting to audition. The production company is Greg Jackson Productions. If you ever saw a cable series called "Close to Famous", about Vegas performers, that was Greg Jackson Productions. It was like a scene out of "Showgirls"and actually, they were auditioning showgirls when I got there, for one of their other shows. Greg was there, a heavyset man in a silk show jacket with "Greg Jackson Production" on the back.

BTW, not to get ahead of myself, but I own one of those.

So they finish with the girls and start calling guys up to the stage to sing. After you sing, they either ask you to stay or thank you and you go on your way. So eventually I hear

"Mr, uhh, Tuuly" Yeah, It's not the first time.

"Yeah, Tully, right here" and I go up on stage.

"What are you going to sing for us today?"

"I'm going to sing "She's a Lady" by Tom Jones"

So I sing it, or most of it, which was more than many of the guys before me. OK. Well at least I wasn't horrible. After I sing, they call me over to the table where the production team is sitting. It's Greg, the director and the choreographer, whose name is "Mistingette", or something like that. No last name.

"So, Robert"

"Bob, please"

"OK, Bob. Do you dance?"

At some point in my life, I think it was when I turned 45 or so, I got comfortable with honesty on this subject.

"No. I don't". And this is where I figured they would thank me for my time and I could get to one of the video poker machines, have Miller lite or 7 and see where the evening takes me. My mistake.

" Well, would you stay for the movement call?"

"Sure. No problem."

So I'm there through the rest of the vocal auditions. It gets down to about a dozen of us. We all get up on stage and we learn a dance combination. Well, some of us learn a dance combination. Some of us learn part of a dance combination. Then we do it all together, then in smaller groups. I'm pretty sure I never got it right. I wasn't the only one who didn't, but there were folks who did. So here is where they thank me for my time and I make up for lost time with the video poker and the Miller.

"Will the following people stay, The rest of you, thank you for your time."

They call 8 names. One of them is mine. I am puzzled and amused. They call us over individually. When they get to me, Greg says "Can you come back next Tuesday? We're going to hold the callbacks then."

"Umm, sure."

What am I going to say? It's a callback for a Vegas show, and I'm an out of work actor. This is what I do, ya know?

"Great. Oh, and bring a different song".

Flash forward to the following Tuesday. I'm back in the theater, now with 10 other prospective Men of Rock. Again, they call us up to sing, one by one. they get to me. I head up to the stage.

"What are you going to sing for us today, my Tuuly?

"I'm going to sing "She's a Lady", by Tom Jones."

Look, it's not like they are going to cast me. Why would I bust my butt to learn a rock song just to sing it once and get cut? And no. They didn't call me on it. We just moved forward. After we all sing they ask 8 of us to stay for another movement call. I swear, 7 of us did the combination. 1 did not. At least not well. At all. So, we are asked to go sit in a certain area. We get called over, one by one. I watch 2 guys get called over & sit down, 3 guys get called over and leave.

"Mr. Tully?" Here it comes. So I go over.

Greg says " Bob, I like your attitude. You're kinda like "Sting"in Guns & Roses."

Umm.... Sting.... Guns & Roses… I'm still trying to do that math when he continues....

"We'd like you to be the "bad boy" of the group. Welcome to "The Men of Rock".

I'm still back on "Sting". I haven't even processed "bad boy"&"Men of Rock" yet. But I do manage to ask a few questions.

"So, (looking at Mistingette, or however it's spelled) what about the dancing?"

"We'll make it work, don't worry about that."

I didn't know what that meant at the time, and it wasn't exactly a truthful response, but I just moved past to the next question.

"So which casino are we playing?. Is it a daytime show here at the Rio?"

"Oh no. The show doesn't play here".

So, umm, which casino are we playing at?"

"You're doing 10 weeks at the 7 Feathers Indian Casino.in Canyonville, Oregon." We rehearse here for 3 weeks and then head up to Southern Oregon for the show."

So here's my thought process. I'm a performer. It's a gig. And it pays decently. It's not forever. And honestly, when will I ever, at 45 years of age, get hired to be part of a glorified boy band? So yeah, I took the job.

Oh, and when Misty said "we'll take care of the dance thing", what she meant was that they would drill me constantly, for hours, day after day, until I kinda got it. After a week I offered to quit and just admit that it was a mistake all around. They talked me into staying, but it was ugly and it was hard.

We played 2 shows a night, six nights a week. It was basically karaoke tracks of rock songs and we were either singing, dancing or backstage changing for the entire hour. The audience was women who were, by and large, middle aged and very, very drunk. We took off our shirts and patches on the back pockets of our pants. They yelled, screamed and threw lingerie. I think that part was ironic, at least most of the time.

Canyonville the town was so small that aside from the casino, there was only 1 bar, which is where we'd go on our off nights. I was once offered home brew there by a guy whose left eye was focused on me & his right eye on the wall to my right. I declined his kind offer. One Monday we went off with the bar staff to a place called "Club 97", which was just off exit 97 of the 5 freeway (Exit number changed to protect, well, someone)

It was a strip club, and the 1 stripper working that night was actually totally nude, in a split on the bar when we arrived. I wondered at that point what we were staying to see, but one of the young ladies our group, a bartender at the casino, evidently was a regular and got up on the bar and stripped, just to mix things up. And that was 10 weeks, in 2005, in Southern Oregon.

And yeah, I did get a "Greg Jackson Productions" silk jacket out of the deal.

23-Corporate America

So I was back in Los Angeles. It was 2005 and I had returned from my Japan adventure and done my 10 weeks in the "Men of Rock". I had picked up a weekend gig as the head coach of a summer beach camp in Corona Del Mar, a beach community down in Orange county. How did an Ohio boy who could barely swim get a job as a head coach of a beach camp for kids?

That's a different story.

But there I was, And I was still working as a company member of a small alternative theater group. In fact I was directing their 1st musical, an adaptation of the musical "Man of La Mancha" and teaching group fitness classes at L.A. Fitness from time to time. So yeah, I was busy.

Busy? Yes.

Rich? Not so much.

I hadn't banked a lot of cash while in Japan, and had spent a lot of that since I had returned to L.A. I was behind on my car payments,. several months behind of my rent, which my landlord had been very gracious about. It helped that I was living in a small back house that he was not, strictly speaking, allowed to rent out, but he was also just a nice guy. However, I couldn't count on the kindness of strangers forever. Beach camp head coach wasn't paying "career type" money, teaching fitness classes about the same, and directing alternative theater was paying exactly what you think it might pay, namely zero. So, what to do to keep the wolf from the door?

A regular gig, that's what. So I started looking.

And in fairly short order stumbled across an ad for a supplement company which gave facility tours. They were looking to expand their tour staff. It was a Mon-Thurs, 9-5 job, and paid decently enough, at least to me it did. So what the heck, I'll apply and see what happens, right?

So began my 15 year journey into Corporate America . Basically, the job was internalizing a 2 hour facility tour, familiarizing yourself with the facility itself, the product line and corporate philosophy. The groups you led were distributors of the products, who either lived locally, or travelled to Los Angeles to visit the facility.

So. Learn lines & blocking, check.

Be relatively entertaining while doing it.Because 2 hours is a long time to just spout info and point to tour highlights. Check.

Espouse the corporate philosophy of fitness and wellness. Check and check-mate.

Let's just say that this was a good fit. But it wasn't going to be a long term thing. Just something to do until I got a good performing gig, right?

Well, the next happy accident occurred when we had several hundred of our top leaders in town for an event which we sponsored, namely the Orange county marathon. There was also a half marathon and 5k run as part of the event. We were a main sponsor for the run, and many of our guests were running . And it was also my first half marathon, paid for by the company. The night before the race, we had a rally for our guests at the host hotel. There were several speakers slated, and I was there just to help support the event, which meant I was basically a "gofer", helping wherever and whenever needed. As it happened, the main speaker, the one that everyone was actually there to see, was running late. None of the execs really wanted to get up, unscripted and unprepared, to cover til he got in the door. One of the execs who knew of me and was aware of my fitness and public speaking background asked me if I would like to "get up and say a few words".

Hello opportunity. Yes, I hear you knocking….

So, in front of most of the top leadership of the corporation, I spent 15 minutes jabbering about wellness, fitness, quality of life and how our supplement line supported all of these things, or something along those lines. I also lead them in cheers, took a running lap around the auditorium while speaking, etc. You know, all of the "let's hype them up until someone gives me the signal that the boss is here & ready".

And hello, what came next? The offer of a regular, salaried job. Nobody from the performing arts world was beating down my door and I kinda liked being able to pay my bills, so I said "Yes".

The next happy accident was that they occasionally needed motivational speakers to give presentations in one of the 65-ish countries which carried our products. And I had just, in a very unofficial and unplanned way, auditioned for that hybrid role.

And that was me, from 2005 until 2021, more or less.

I wrote tour scripts, I hired and trained new people. I was the boss of about a dozen staff. And every once in a while, I would travel as a motivational & informational speaker. I got to create presentations, which appealed to my theatrical little heart. Many of my trips were in support of company sponsored health and fitness events. I ran races in Denmark, Amsterdam, Singapore & Indonesia. Other adventures as well, but those are separate stories.

I was, not for the 1st or last time, lucky.

When people asked me what I did for a living, I would just say marketing. The truth was that a role was created for me that fit my talents. Did I love all of it? Of course not. There is a class consciousness in the corporate environment that I don't really support or enjoy. And I missed performing.

And both of those things were just me, whining…

That period of my life did a lot for me. Financially, it took me out of a hole and put me back on my feet. It exposed me to people from every corner of the world. And let me experience places I would never have gotten to otherwise. I worked with and learned from some amazing people. I formed lifetime friendships.

This chapter of my life came to an end in late 2020, partially due to COVID, partially because of changes in the job itself. And I don't regret stepping away, moving back to where I grew up and the unexpected renaissance in my performing life.

But those 15 years had their interesting moments…

Me looking all Corporate..

24-Kickboxing in Manila

Kicking it in the Philippines.

As related in other stories, yeah, I got to travel a fair bit as a speaker and trainer for my corporate gig. Did all of those gigs go as planned?

Do they ever?

-Like the time I had to teach a fitness class in China, at 8am, outdoors in 30 degrees, the day after a late night of cocktailing with our Chinese associates. We were doing shots of what they called white wine. In this case, white wine was a euphemism for their moonshine, which I described at the time

119

as tasting like it had been distilled in a urinal. I didn't say that to them, of course. I took one for the team. Or 5 or 6 for the team, to be exact. To their credit, all of my Chinese associates, who drank way more than I did, turned up at my class the next morning, though several visited a bush in the back of the square. Some more than once.

-Or the time in Portland where my Taiwanese guests were fascinated with the chopper motorcycles parked outside of our hotel. Fascinated enough to actually get on the bikes and start taking pictures of each other, as I pleaded with them to stop. Then I took a turn pleading with the bike's owners when they came out and discovered the impromptu photo op.

-Then there was the 5k race organized by our affiliate in Indonesia. It was actually the only race I have ever outright won. Or at least I think I did. The folks who put the race together had their hearts in the right place, but weren't terribly versed in race organization. When I came around the last corner what I saw were the hosts of the event. What I didn't see was a finish line. They just said "You can stop now". That's a lot less satisfying than busting through a tape, just so you know. And there was the trip to Africa, but that deserves its own story. The one I want to talk about here & now was a speaking tour of Southeast Asia.

I was traveling with several VIPs, and one of our stops was Manila, Philippines. The folks putting the tour together asked me if it was true I taught kick-boxing back at home. My reply was;

"Yes, I do teach cardio-kickboxing back in the states."

"Oh great! Would you be willing to lead a group as part of our wellness fair at the Mall of Asia"?

The Mall of Asia is the largest shopping mall in the Philippines, and the location of the event.

"Oh, OK. As long as I've got a way to play my music & folks are ready and willing to participate, why not?"

"Yes! They will love that!"

I am nothing if not accommodating. Comes the day of the event. I arrive at the venue in the afternoon. The big event, where I'm speaking, along with our VIPs, isn't until the evening, but this is part of the build up, so I'm the only one from my group in attendance. The VIPs are back at the hotel, sipping cocktails with Hillary Clinton, who was First Lady at the time. Well, Hillary was there and they were there. I don't know about the cocktails.

But I'm at the mall, watching the other acts they have booked for the event. And it would seem that all of the other acts are actual martial artists. Not aerobic instructors. These were actual, board-breaking, bone-breaking martial artists. And the audience? Yes, many of them are distributors of our products. That's a plus. But they are in suits and ties, dressed for business. They are ready for a cocktail party. Or photo ops with the VIPs. What they are NOT dressed for is a short cardio-kickboxing class. Like the one I was about to teach. I have visions in my head. Visions of me up on a stage, where people have just watched real martial artists, doing my cutesy little aerobic routine. Alone.

What to do? Tell them I've suddenly gotten ill and need to go back to the hotel? Feign sunstroke? Throw myself down a flight of stairs? All of this went through my mind. What I decided on, in my naiveté, was honesty.

"Look, I think there has been a misunderstanding. I'm not a martial artist. I teach cardio classes. These people aren't dressed to take a class and there is no reason for me to go up there alone. If we can just cancel my appearance and I'll come back tonight and speak."

"No, Mr Bob. They will love you. They have seen your videos and are looking forward to your appearance. We have already told them that you are the finale to this afternoon's event."

Yes, I've done promotional videos for the brand. Dammit.

At this point I just figure I'm probably never going to be in the Philippines again. I'll just make an ass of myself here, then move along with my life.. Kind of like when you're wading into a cold pool and you're up to your thighs. This next part is gonna suck, but then it will be over.

So, I go up, They introduce me, and I signal for the music to start…and 20 or 30 of the people in the audience get up and join me on stage. Some take off their jacket, some remove their high heels. In their collared shirts and ties and dresses and pantsuits, they get up on stage. And we do 20 mins of cardio. The audience gets into it as much as they can from their chairs. People walking by, who have nothing to do with the event, start doing some of the moves in the mall aisle ways.

Aside from the massive relief, all I can think of is "this would never happen back home". I think that there is a simple happiness and enjoyment of life there that I think our concern with image and being "cool" robs us of. I saw it that day in the Philippines. I also saw it in Japan, when I worked there. And I was amazed. And grateful.

Sometimes life just works out. All you gotta do is put it out there and trust in the universe.

8am. 30 degrees. China

25-Africa

There was one particular assignment during my corporate years that deserves it's own piece. This particular gig was hosting a VIP group going to Zambia. We would go to Lusaka, the capitol, to show them some of the charity work that they were financing, then take them to Victoria Falls, the largest waterfall in the world. Vic Falls spans the border between Zambia and Zimbabwe, but we were staying on the Zambia side.

A memorable event. With memorable adventures;

Adventure #1- Giraffes

At Victoria Falls, our clients were staying at an amazing hotel, right at the falls. We, the staff, were staying at a less amazing, but still very cool hotel right next to the amazing one. The 2 hotels were joined by a walkway about a half mile long. On the grounds of both hotels, many animals wandered freely. Not all animals. Like lions weren't allowed, or elephants, though elephants were kept out by a fence that I'm not really sure would have stopped a determined german shepherd, but I'm no expert. So on any given day, taking a walk of the grounds, you could encounter antelope, monkeys, zebras....and giraffes.

I know, I know. Giraffes are herbivores. They don't eat meat, much less people. And we've seen the images of people feeding giraffes. However, I have also watched enough Mutual of Omaha's Wild Kingdoms to know that they can also kick in a lions ribcage .

Thank you Marlin Perkins.

So one evening, when my co-worker Sheri and I were walking back from the amazing hotel to our cool hotel, we turn a corner and there are 3 giraffes, right in the middle of the path. The path was about 10 ft wide, and the giraffes were grouped together, munching on leaves in the surrounding trees. This is a very cool sight. No cages, no bars, no zoo-keepers. Just us. And the giraffes. However….

We have to get past them. Which at this point would involve literally sliding around their legs, underneath them. Here's where the whole lion's ribcage thing starts to hit home with me. So Sheri and I decide to wait it out for a minute.

"Maybe they'll move on"

"Yeah, maybe"

So we back up about 10 ft and wait for a few minutes. Then one of the giraffes moves so there's about a 10 foot gap on one side. And I decide that that's as good an opportunity as we are likely to get, so I give her a look, which I am under the impression she understands as "let's go".

I go. Shari doesn't.

I get past, but as I do, the giraffe kinda steps back into its original space, so the gap is gone. But now Shari is committed to going, so she weaves between giraffe legs and makes it through. Up until now the giraffes have basically ignored us. But at this point, having these 2 corporate types, in polo shirts, weaving through their legs has sort of captured their attention. So they turn and start walking toward us, bending their heads down.

Yeah, I know what you're saying you would have done. Picked some leaves from a tree, fed the giraffes, had a "one with nature" moment, took pictures….

Yeah, sure.

Neither Sheri nor I even entertained the idea. We backed up, they followed, we walked, they followed. We then broke into a dead run. Luckily Sheri was also an athlete, so I wasn't abandoning her. Don't ask me what would have happened if she wasn't. Of course they could have caught us if it mattered to them, but it didn't. We did a quick 100 yards, slowed up, looked back and started cracking up. Chased by giraffes. So there's that.

Adventure #2 Baboons

The next day I was checking out walking paths around the falls. There are paths that crisscross the entire area, and I wanted to take the group on a hike. So I'm walking down a series of steps leading to a viewing area and as I turn a corner there are 5 or 6 baboons, hanging out on the staircase. Again, no bars, no keepers, just baboons. Hanging out on the stairs. Now, unlike giraffes, baboons don't have what you would call a pristine reputation. Huge strength, big teeth, unpredictable mood. I decide that discretion is the better part of valor on this one. I'm going to go back the way I came, slowly.

One problem.

Two other baboons have appeared just up the stairway, the way I came. I suddenly feel like a Shark who stumbled into Jet territory. Except I don't think we'll be doing any choreography. And Officer Krupke won't be breaking things up.

The two above me are directly on the path. Going down, the half dozen are more by the stairs, and one is kinda hanging on the guard rail, but there's a gap. I move as slowly as I have ever moved in my life, walking down past them, muttering to myself "Please, oh please" Just that. I'm not even sure what I was asking for. Maybe just a hall pass. And as I passed the one on the rail I could have reached out and shaken his hand. And he could have taken that hand, torn my arm off and beaten me over the head with it. So I didn't. And he didn't.

Adventure #3 - Zebras

It was not the fault of the Zebra. It definitely wasn't.

I had abandoned the idea of an unguided nature hike in favor of a 5k jog along the path between the hotels. Kind of a morning "wake me up". And the VIPs were all fitness focused so they loved the idea. As we are running the path we pass 3 zebras, 2 adults and a very young baby zebra. In fact it had been born the previous day, as I found out later. Very cute. I was leading the group, and Sheri was at the back, playing sweeper, keeping everyone together. After I've passed the zebras I hear Sheri saying "No, I don't think you want to…" then the sound of an impact. I turn just in time to see one of our guests bounce off the wall of a building, which is what you would do if you were kicked by a zebra. Which is what a zebra mom will do if you decide to try to take a "selfie" with mom and baby zebra. Luckily, and through no merit of his own, the guest was unharmed except for some sore ribs. And Sheri & I kept our jobs. But that leads me to …

Adventure #4 VIPs

There is a bridge over the river leading to Victoria Falls. The river separates Zambia & Zimbabwe. It is also the home of the 7th highest bungie jump in the world. And the VIP of the VIP group. one of the highest ranking distributors in the world, multimillionaire and personal friend of every bigwig in our corporate world, wanted to jump off that bridge. With his entire team of 5 . He told us that as soon as we met him at the start of the event. Len was 70 years old. Yes he was athletic. Yes he was an Ironman competitor, But no, we were NOT fans of this idea and during the multi-day event we did everything we could to dissuade him.

So on the 2nd last day he pulled us aside and said " I know that this concerns you. I know that you're worried about our safety. But whether you like it or not, with or without your help, we are going to jump off that bridge." So, I said " OK, let me check out what's involved and we'll set it up, if we can". He says, "Good. I'll go with you". Like I would have made up some flimsy excuse as to why we couldn't do it, Like equipment failure. Or an obscure African holiday. Which is exactly what I planned on doing.

So we go and set it up. And as we are making our reservations, Len says "I'm paying for everybody. And if you two want to jump, I'll pay for you too." My response?

"Well in that case Len, I'll jump. Because if anything happens to you, I might as well jump, with or without the cord".

So the next day, there we are. A last little twist was that since the middle of the bridge was a border between the 2 countries, the Zambian authorities, located in a tiny guard shack right before the bridge, asked for "someone's passport" before we could pass.

I gave them mine. At that point I had a sort a fatalistic attitude anyway. One of the guests I was hosting might plummet to their death, or Sheri and I to ours. So my passport ends up being sold in a black market in Zambia. Big deal. I'll probably be dead or a fugitive anyway.

So we all walk to the 2 pop up tents which are tied together, which is the actual setup on the bridge. I watch Len and all of his people jump, then they tie my legs together with towels, attach the bungie cord, and I literally walk a plank overlooking this drop. BTW, that's the scariest part. Standing on a plank looking down into what looks like a tiny river surrounded by rocks.

"5,4,3,2,1" And I jump.

It was both exhilarating, and terrifying.

And I tore my right meniscus. But it was worth it.

Oh, and the next day, while trying to take a group photo at our farewell dinner, one of the guests fell into a bonfire.

Dead. Solid. Perfect.

Waiting to jump. The smile is fake.

26-Jericoacoara

Jeri

I have a favorite place in the world

Jericoacoara.

Jericoacoara, or "Jeri", as we'll refer to it moving forward, is a tiny town in the Northeastern Brazil. It's remote. The 2 times I've been there, it had no airport. It does now, though it's also tiny. It also has no paved roads. It's all sand and dirt. It's on the coast of the Atlantic, so there's the beach and sand dunes. Like, Saudi Arabia sand dunes.

It's about a 4-5 hour drive from the nearest major city, which is Fortaleza. The last hour of the trip is where the sand starts. So you either have to deflate your tires and hope you can find the correct path through the dunes to the town, or hire a jeep to finish the drive for you. Once you get to Jeri, it's just small boutique hotels, restaurants, stores, etc. No Hilton, no Hooters, no Starbucks....

...just Paradise.

How did I end up in a remote town in N.E. Brazil? Fair question. The company I worked for had a farm in another N.E. Brazilian town called Ubajara. I was there with my boss, scouting the farm and surrounding area for an event we wanted to put for some VIP guests. At the end of our last day at the farm, the farm manager, a very cool guy named Joao, insisted that we stay the night in Jeri before we flew out of Fortaleza back to the states. And he insisted to our "keeper", Willem, the young man who was conducting us throughout our visit, that we get there "before sunset". Joao wouldn't say why, which lead to us questioning what happened in Jeri after the sun went down. But we agreed to stay there, and off we went. When you're not really sure of the "why" in what you're doing, it can lead to some interesting conversations.

So eventually, after switching to the jeep and weaving through countless sand dunes, there it is. Jericoacoara. It's almost sunset, and we see a line of folks walking out of the town itself, up the large dune right next to it. Willem says "We'll stop the jeep, get out, and they will take our stuff to the hotel." So we exit the jeep and follow the people up the sand dune. This is what Joao wanted us to be a part of. At the end of the day, everybody goes to the top of the dune and watches the sunset. There are vendors selling drinks and snacks, some people have some music playing & you sit there and enjoy an amazing sunset. So that's what we did. Beer in hand. Music. People chatting or laughing or just watching, in silence.

Afterwards we walked down to the town, along the beach, where people were performing capoeira, the Brazilian martial art that is almost a dance in itself. On the main path into the center of town, you walk through a phalanx of drink carts, where vendors compete to sell you caipirinhas. That's a combination of cachaca, the Brazilian version of moonshine, combined with fruit, sugar & ice. Did we comparison shop? Oh yes we did.

Jeri is also a windsurfing mecca. It's cool to watch. No, I didn't try it. I've learned enough about things that involve balance & coordination. I'll tell you sometimes about my attempt at skim boarding. But that's a different story.

And, honestly, that's Jericoacoara.

Beach

Sun

Surfing

Sunsets

Caipirinhas

Dunes

Seafood

Tropical fruits

Amazing stars at night

Oh, and hippies. And ganja. That should actually be understood when I say surfing and remote beaches, but I want to paint the whole picture. A person in our group called me aside to go back to the beach/vendor area because she saw a stand that had some amazingly cool pipes. After she made her purchase she offered to "break it in" with me.

So, we're there in Jeri. The decision is made that we really need to take an extra day there to "explore all of the possibilities of the place, guest experience-wise".

Unanimous agreement.

We were going to end our visit with a nice dinner at one of the local restaurants. This being the tail end of an 8 day trip, my clothes are, well, ripe. I don't even like being around myself in most of my clothes, much less in the company of others. So I decide to go buy a shirt. So I'm walking through the main square, shopping, and I see a clothing shop. Kind of light, linen-ish clothing. Perfect. I walk in and start looking around. The only other people in the store are a couple.

She is a beautiful woman.

He is, as far as I can tell, Fabio.

Not actually Fabio. But he has the beautiful long hair, the chiseled features, the tan toned physique. Also he's not wearing a shirt or shoes. I'm not sure what aspect of his life I'm more jealous of, but I let that go. I'm here for a shirt. And then he addresses me.

"My friend, can I help you". With a latin accent. Of course.

"Umm, I'm looking for a shirt. Have you seen a clerk or anything?"

"My friend, this is my store". He says a few words to the beautiful woman in Spanish and she leaves. At this point I feel bad that I have interrupted what looked like a commercial for a Sandals resort.

"I'm sorry. I can come back.."

"No, it's alright. Are you American?"

"Yes, you?

"I am from Argentina". Yeah, that too….

He continues….

Why are you here in Jericoacoara?" When he says "Jericoacoara", it sounds like music.

"I'm here for work"

"Then you must come back. And you will sit on the beach and watch the stars and drink the cachaca. This you must do."

This from Fabio, with an accent, no shirt or shoes, in his store. I'm heterosexual. I know this from 60 years of experience. But damn….

I pick a shirt. He gives me the life history of the shirt. How it was made, how to care for it, where the fabric is from. I am sold, and would probably have bought anything else he wanted to sell me. But we left it there.

The 2nd time we went back to Jeri, about a year later, the shop was gone. But the vibe was still there. We ate seafood while sitting on a bench with our feet in the water the food was caught in. The rode dune buggies and slid down sand dunes.

And watched the sunset.

And drank the cachaca.

And yeah, it's on my bucket list. To go back there and spend more time in my paradise, on my own dime. in my own time.

And I still own that shirt.

Sunset in Jericoacoara

27-The Price Hill in Me

Price Hill was a long time ago for me, in many ways. In years of course, but also, well, culturally. Since then I've had a long term love affair with performing arts. I've been exposed to, and accepted, many different cultures and customs. I've lived where Americans are a minority, and sometimes an oddity. I've seen our country through the eyes of people who don't necessarily accept us or like us. As a heterosexual man in performing arts I've often been in the minority. I've seen prejudice in many forms, against many different groups. I think I have learned to live and let live. I really do value the experiences and I know they have changed me. A lot.

But down there, at my core, there is still Price Hill. My Price Hill. The Price Hill of my youth. There are still values and basic philosophies that I don't think will ever change. And from time to time it asserts itself;

- I was in Amsterdam a work trip. Ran a race called the "Dam to Dam". If you're a runner and you get a chance, do it. Bands all along the route, which goes through villages from Amsterdam to Zaandam. And I don't mean suburbs. I mean villages. Cobblestone streets, bars with their speakers outside, playing music, people offering you beers. A great run in general. After we get done, several co-workers and I walk down through the red light district. After returning what I thought was an open-handed wave from several of the girls, I was told that they weren't waving, they were letting me know that 50 euros was the basic price for their services. Oops, my mistake. So later that evening we return to our hotel. As we are walking in, a couple of the guys grab my shoulder, hold me up and tell me that they are going back to the district.

I'm single. I've got 50 euros. Maybe even a few more. There is nothing stopping me.

Except…

Price Hill.

Where I'm from it seems like somebody is being taken advantage of. And if the girl, no matter how gorgeous she is (and some of them were) is only doing it for my 50 euro, why am I doing it in the first place? And I honestly feel that way. Have all of my life. It's not morality. I don't think I'm a judge of that. I think it's just where I'm from and how I was raised. So nope, I actually went to a bar overlooking the main strip of the district, sat on a balcony seat, drank my Heinekins and watched the business of that business. And THAT, my friends, was an entertaining evening.

-I went to Phuket Thailand to run a half marathon which, btw, damn near killed me. 13.1 miles which started at 5:30 am at 80 degrees and 80% humidity. Brutal. But after the race, I moved from my hotel near the race route to a different hotel at Patong beach, which is party central for Phuket. I mean, if you're going to go, you at least want to see what all the fuss is about, right? So I go out for the evening, have some beers, find a cute bartender with tattoos and an attitude, which is a favorite weakness of mine no matter where I am in the world, drink some overpriced shots and beers with her, then get up my courage and go into one of the "clubs". It's 10pm-ish, still very early by local standards, so there aren't many customers.

Girls? Yes, there were a lot of those. Not a lot of clothing, but yeah, a lot of girls. And aside from the bartender there, who spoke a little English, it was all Thai, all the time. I had on cargo shorts (go figure) and they were fascinated with my Celtic cross tattoo. They were joking amongst themselves about it.

But at one point, it was apparent that I was supposed to make a choice. I don't think it had to be a single choice, but a selection was expected.

Price Hill.

What I did was buy a few rounds of drinks for the girls, we worked around our language barrier and their confusion, had some laughs and I took my leave. The next morning I got in a taxi and went back to my hotel near the race route (it was a really nice hotel, ya'll), enjoyed 2 more days of beach, sun, and a small shack of a beach bar with a little man dressed only in shorts who offered you peanuts and cigarettes when you bought a beer. I hung out there and flew home 2 days later.

-I was on a cruise, hanging with a great group of friends from a prior cruise. It was Halloween night. My friends were going down to the dance club, where we ended most nights, but I wanted to stay upstairs for the deck party, so I told them I'd meet them later. There was a light rain, but it was the Caribbean, it was Halloween, I'd had a cocktail or 3 and there was good music so I was dancing. I do that on cruises. A girl who I'd seen hanging around with our group came up to me, danced with me for a while and said ;

"You're Bob, right?"

"Yup, hi."

"Hi. I'm Debbie (or something). You're with the group, right"?

"Yeah"

"Are you with somebody?"

Debbie (or something) was very cute.

"Nope, just partying with the group"

"I've got a question. I picked up some "stuff" on the island today. I came on the ship with some people but they are jerks and I'm looking for somebody to share this stuff with. Have you got your own room?

Just FYI. I always get my own room. I love everyone, but at the end of the night I want to have my own space. If you know me that makes sense. So...

"Yes, I do"

"Can we meet up there in say a half hour?"

OK. So here is my thought process. Bringing any drugs onto or off a cruise ship is incredibly stupid. However, she's already done the dumb part. She brought the pot onboard. And you constantly smell ganja in the hallways of the ship. I'm not a regular pot smoker, but I have, it's a cruise, and Debbie is really cute. So...

I tell her my room number and make the date, if you will.

30 minutes later I'm in my room. There's a knock at the door. Debbie.

She comes in. I offer her a drink.

I'm having Miller lite. Big surprise, I know.

She takes a drink, sits down and pulls out what looks like a travel size Ibuprofen bottle. You know, one of those tiny tubes that holds like 10 tablets. She proceeds to tap out 2 line of cocaine.

Oh. Well. This is a different kettle of fish entirely. I've never done coke. Again, not a moral thing. It's just not been a priority for me. But here is the perfect opportunity. No one but Debbie would know. I don't have to be anywhere for, say, 4 days. If I ever wanted to go down this road...?

Price Hill

"You know what. I think that's for you. I'm happy with my Miller Lite".

I think my drug of choice is alcohol. Bad beer, good wine. And I'm not really all that curious to try new things designed to mess with my mind. If I can't get it over the bar at the Crow's Nest, I probably don't want it.

…except for wine. I haven't seen the wine list at the Crow's Nest but I'm a wine snob. So shoot me.

To tie this all into a neat little bow, I think that adults are free to make their own choices. And I am free to make mine. Which I think are linked to my youth. And my neighborhood. I think there's a cliche that covers this.

You can take the boy out of Price Hill but….

…well, you know the rest.

Patong Beach

My beach bartender
(I gave him the shirt)

28-2AM, New Orleans

In the early 2010s I got my butt kicked in a New Orleans hotel at 2am .

It was one of the better experiences of my life.

It's not what you're thinking.

I'll explain.

I've never been a fighter. Growing up in my neighborhood, fist fights were a way of life. Getting into a beef at school and going to "the hollow" to settle matters was a semi-regular occurrence. But not for me. I didn't often get into that kind of disagreement, but when I did, I would back down.

Simply put, I was afraid. In a small enclosed environment like an elementary school, you got to know everyone pretty well. You know who were the tough guys, who were the bullies, and who were the victims. I was one of the latter. There was a bully in our neighborhood. I had chances to stand up to him but I never did. I was bullied, I watched other people get bullied. And I never stepped in.

I carried that with me for most of my life. I think that was a major source of disappointment for my father. Dad was handy with his fists. He would fight at the drop of a hat. We heard stories about him from uncles and family friends. The one time we talked about it, he said it was a matter of proving he was tough enough to take whatever someone else could dish out. And I don't think he could understand, or certainly not respect, that the thought of fighting scared me.

And after growing up as the butt of jokes about my weight, etc. and being bullied myself, as an adult I could never stand seeing other people being bullied. Adults don't default immediately to violence, so I would step in to stand up for people if I thought they were being victimized. Several times things would get to the brink of something physical, but it never got there. I wouldn't back down, but I always wondered what I would do if it came to violence.

Which takes me to New Orleans. I was there to get on a cruise ship. Another singles cruise. I was at the pre-cruise party, the night before, to meet up with friends and pick up whatever booze we were going to smuggle on the ship. You know, the basics. So we had the pre-cruise party at the hotel and then, being in the Big Easy, we went out on the town. Cocktails, dancing, meeting new folks, the whole 9 yards. Great evening.

So I'm heading back to the hotel at about 2:00-2:30. Tired, sweaty, more than a little drunk. I'll shower, set my alarm for the morning to catch the cab for the ship, etc. I get into the elevator and go up to my floor. The elevator door opens and I hear a commotion. To my left is my room. To my right, down the hall, 3 really drunk people I know are having a loud, mean argument.

I've cruised with these people before. He's a big, loud, former military dude. Not really my cup of tea but we know each other. They are yelling , pushing, shoving, screaming…

I've got a choice here.

I can just turn to my left, walk to my room and avoid the whole issue. I'm not here with them, didn't even know they were coming on the cruise. Not my circus, not my monkeys. But, he's being abusive. Verbally and physically.

Ah hell.

So I turn right, with every intention of de-escalating the situation. One problem.

Actually, 2 problems.

Problem #1 I'm drunk

Problem #2 I have a smart mouth.

So I get between him and them. He says some things. I say some things. He punches me in the mouth. I fall down. He gets on top of me and puts his hands around my throat. You know that move they always tell you to do when someone has their hands around your throat, where you bring your arms up through his and knock his hands away?

Yeah, I didn't think of that.

What I thought was " dammit, I still can't fight worth a darn, and he may be about to kill me, here in a hotel in New Orleans".

Well, that didn't happen. The girls yelled at him to stop, I guess he realized that killing me would be, well, inconvenient, and he stopped choking me. I didn't go the police, etc. One, because the girls begged me not to. Also, if I did I would be blowing off a several thousand dollar cruise.

And 3 days later, on the cruise, I came across the 3 of them drunk in a bar and the best of friends. They even asked me over and offered me a drink. Seems that this was a cyclical thing. Party, get drunk, argue, get violent, makeup. I was just sort of collateral damage.

No, I didn't take them up on their kind offer. I've actually never seen them since. But that's not the point. The point was that I could have turned left. It would have been the safe choice. And as it turned out, the smart choice. But I didn't. I chose to try to help, even though I knew that it could turn out, well, the way it turned out. I don't care that I got my butt kicked.

I stood up. I didn't walk away.

I've always been happy about that.

29-Mom

Eileen Charlotte O'Donnell

I wrote this right after Mom passed from dementia in 2019.

Eileen Charlotte O'Donnell was born in 1939 on the west side of Cincinnati. Her mom was an American girl of Irish descent. Her dad was an O'Donnell from Donegal. Dad passed on early in Eileen's life, so she grew up in a household with her grandparents, my Great-Grandma & Grampa Ritter. Great Grandma "read the cards", kinda like a fortune teller.

Mom went to Catholic grade school & Elizabeth Seton Catholic girl's high school, located right next to Archbishop Elder Catholic boys high school, which is where yours truly barely graduated many years later. Eileen did what you were supposed to do in that place at that time. She met an Elder boy, fell in love, got married and had kids. Five of them to be exact. And I expect that she figured her life course was set at that point. Stay on the west side, stay married, raise the kids, have a crop of grandkids, etc. Because that's what you did in that place, at that time.

Then the script got flipped. She found herself divorced, with 5 kids, a high school diploma and no work experience. That wasn't supposed to happen. I can't imagine how afraid she must have been, how uncertain the future looked. She got help, but on a day to day basis she was raising five kids and trying to earn decent money. And you know what?

She did it.

She got a job with a large company. She worked there. She raised us kids. And you know what else she did?

She lived her life. She got involved in her Irish culture. She participated in Irish-American organizations, rising to the office of National Vice President in the Hibernians. She traveled to her homeland in Ireland. And she shared that love with her kids. Four of us actually competed in Irish dance. (guess which one wasn't quite co-ordinated enough.) We spend many weekends immersed in Irish music, dance & culture. I don't think all five of us dug it completely, or to the same extent, but I know for me it opened my eyes to other cultures in general. Since then I have had a love affair with travel and other countries, people and lifestyles. Eileen gave me that.

I have been accused of not needing much of an excuse to throw a party, or open a bottle. That's because the leaf didn't fall far from the tree on that one either. I remember several situations in my teens where I nervously snuck in the house at 2 am, and Mom snuck in at 3.

She enjoyed her life. She loved, and was loved. She taught me how to throw a party, at least the kind of party I like. Things didn't have to be pretty. Our house was usually in disarray, which we frantically tried to "deshambolize" before people arrived. That wasn't important. It was important to have at least twice as much food as your guests could possibly consume, and a well-stocked bar. If Mom had shoes on, they didn't stay on long, which prompted my Uncle to call her a "hillbilly". The party would career from stories to jokes to arguments to tears, like any good Irish party should.

Eileen put up with a lot from the five of us. We could be a pretty wild bunch. I was definitely no bargain. But she accepted us as we were. She actually took in strays from time to time. Friends of ours who needed a place to stay. She didn't have the time. She didn't have the funds. But she did it anyway. Her acceptance of us extended throughout our lives. She never stopped worrying about us, and trying to help us. She spent money she couldn't afford to spend without a second thought. Her selflessness amazed me. She accepted and loved her children's spouses and the families that grew from these unions. When my brother's boys played football, she lived and died with their teams. She never had that experience with her children, though she did actually cry in the stands the one time I pitched in a little league baseball game. I was that bad. True story.

Other Eileen facts;

-She was the best cook I ever met. From sauerkraut & sausage to pot roast to goetta, to the cheesecake that has made me into the cheesecake snob that I am today. She was the best, hands down.

-She once, after the dissolution of yet another relationship of mine, told me that "if I was gay, it was alright".

-Her favorite Irish song was "4 Green Fields" .

-She taught me that you can be a strong person, and yet cry at the drop of a hat.

Over the years, when I would visit Cincinnati, it never failed that when I was leaving, she would cry. I would try to crack jokes, or laugh, or remind her that "I'll be back in ...." . But still she would cry. She knew I needed to go. She knew it was time, and I was happier going back to wherever I was, and doing whatever crazy project, show or job I was doing. And she was happy for me, knowing that I was happy. Didn't matter. She'd still end up watching me go with tears in her eyes.

So now it's my turn.

I know she needs to go. I know damn well that where she is going will be a better place, and that the last year here has been, frankly, horrific. I know that she will be happier, and I am happy for her. But I will say goodbye with tears in my eyes. Tears of happiness that this last part of her journey is over. Tears of sadness that I won't be able to share my life with her, and make her laugh at my foolishness. Safe travels Mom. And to paraphrase an old Irish blessing;

Until we meet again, may God hold you in the palm of his Hand.

30-In the Background

Background work. Also known as being an "extra".

It's something that I think everyone who has tried to get into the business has at least dipped their metaphorical toe in. I've dipped several, at various times. I've never actually enjoyed it, though I've met several celebrity types while on set. A few things bother me about the extra life.

First is, you're not an actor.

I know this because they tell you that, point blank. There are areas for cast, for crew and for background. They are not the same. You sit separate from cast & crew, you eat either at a separate place from cast & crew, or, if it's the same area, after they have finished. There is a caste system, and you are at the bottom of it. You sit for hours on end, just for the opportunity of, maybe, getting on set. Then when you are on set you are considered, as one clever person put it, "scenery that eats". Not a moniker I would choose.

There were 2 separate times when I gave background work the old college try. The first time was in the late 80's when I first got into town and was trying to find my way. The 2nd was in 2021 after I left my corporate job and thought, "maybe it's changed, or I've changed."

It hadn't and I hadn't.

And also, in my case, because I've never done the job long enough to accumulate the credits to become a SAG (Screen Actor's Guild) background artist, I was even at the bottom of the extras queue.

I don't function well like that.

In 2021, when I was trying to once again convince myself I could do background work, I took a background gig on a production called "The Dropout" about the Theranos scandal. Amanda Seyfried starred in it.

Since it was a 5:30 am call in West L.A., I also took a gig in a metal band video shoot starting at 10:00 pm in the valley. No way they were going to keep us there over 12 hours.

Oh my naivete.

In the "Dropout" shoot I got placed at the security desk and once I was placed there they just kept me there for continuity, throughout the shooting day. And no, if they ever had me in frame, it never made it to the final cut. But they had to get a certain number of scenes shot during that day so we shot until 8:00-ish. Then, after we wrapped, I had to return the costumes and have the costume people approve that I had done it correctly, then get in line to get my pay voucher signed. It was a long line, but by the time I got to the front of the line I had just enough time to get the signature, jump in my car and get to the valley, where they were shooting the video. And then…

One of the PAs (production assistants) in charge of the extras says "Wait, are there non-union extras in this line? I need all union extras to step to the front of the line and non-union to line up behind them".

At this point I'm 2nd in line.

Nope.

I throw the voucher down (yeah, I threw it.) on the table, look at the PA and say "I've got a shoot in the valley. I don't have time for this", turn and walk away. Not something you want to do if you're aiming to get additional work. Or get paid. But again, I'm not good with being a 2nd, 3rd or 4th class citizen.

So I run to the car, get to the valley just in time, get made up like a zombie and shoot until dawn. Just FYI, the band is called Ice Nine Kills, the video was "Rainy Day and I appear around the 1:36 point. Zombie.

On another shoot, which was for the series "Obi Wan", I did have a short conversation with the star, Ewen McGregor. We were on set and had just finished shooting a scene. I was a blue alien (side story about that in a minute) . Ewen was walking off set and, as he walked by me, a tissue dropped out of his pocket and fell on the floor. My thought wasn't "Oh, here's a chance to talk to Ewen McGregor". My thought was "If a P.A. sees that tissue, the background people are going to get a 10 minute lecture about bringing things on set". So I said;

"Excuse me"

Ewen, stopped, looked at me; "Yes"

"I don't know if it's important or not, but that just fell out of your, uh, robe"

"It did?"

"Yeah"

"Oh" And he picked it up and walked away.

That was whole conversation.

Blue alien add on story. I told that story when I was backstage during a production of "White Christmas"in Springboro, Ohio, a year later, One of my cast mates said;

" You were in "Obi-Wan?"

"I was on set. I don't think it even made it to the final cut".

"You were a blue alien?"

"Yeah"

"What was the scene like?"

I gave him a basic idea of who was in the scene and what the set looked like. and about 2 mins later he says "There you are!" and shows me, on his phone, the 1 second of me crossing frame as a blue alien in "Obi-Wan."

Some people really like their Star Wars.

31-Ragnar Breakup

Several subjects.

First, the marvelous experience that is a Ragnar relay.

Also, unique break ups.

So. To begin, Ragnar relays are simply that. Relay running races. That's the picture of me running a Ragnar several chapters ago. I got introduced to them via a friend who asked me to join her team for a SoCal Ragnar. The SoCal (Southern California) Ragnar is the classic road version. It starts in Huntington Beach and finishes in San Diego, a distance of approximately 200 miles. A regular team is 12 people, each of whom will run 3 legs. A leg can vary from 3 miles to, well, the longest leg I ever ran was 12 miles. Almost a half marathon. And then I had 2 more legs to run after that. You get 2 vans, cram runners #1-6 in van1 and 7-12 in van 2 . Runner 1 starts their leg, the vans drive to the 1st transfer point, where runner 1 passes off the slap bracelet to runner #2. Then the vans go to transfer #2, where runner 2 passes to runner 3, and so on through transfer 36. We'd start on a Friday morning and end up in San Diego on Saturday afternoon. And yes, it's continuous. You could have a leg to run at 2am. You're sleeping as best you can in the back of a van, with music, sweaty runners and smelly runner clothing, snacking on protein bars, bananas, gatorade, beer, whatever works for you. I did 2 of those. There's also a trail Ragnar, which is usually in a park or wooded area. There are 3 trails and 8 team members, with each runner doing all 3 trails. You bring tents or campers or just sleeping bags. There's a central "village" where there is usually a fire, a main tent with food, drinks and swag for sale. I did 2 or those as well. And then there was a Ragnar "sprint" which was 6 people, 2 legs each, from Ft. Lauderdale to Miami. I put together my own team for that, Team "Built for Comfort, not for Speed", which was our commentary on overly competitive teams. We had a ball on that one, so naturally they have never offered it again. Oh well…..

Around that same time I started dating a girl named Cara. (sure, close enough). We met at an Irish fair in Long Beach. Very cute girl. Very successful woman. A runner as well, which was cool. She was in upper management for a pharmaceutical company, so, yes, Cara was doing pretty well. She had 2 boys from a previous marriage. And we got along very well, to start.

Now I'll give you my version of what turned out to be our fatal flaw. I'm quite sure that Cara's version would be different. And the truth would lie somewhere between.

My version is that Cara was used to running things. As a director, she ran things on the job. She ran her immediate family, as the sole parent. She ran her extended family because of the money she made. She would organize family vacations to vacation homes in Malibu, for example. Yeah, I went with them for New Years. Where we watched Dick Clark's Rocking New Year's Eve with Ryan Seacrest. In Malibu. With a beautiful beach and the Pacific ocean right outside our door.

Whatever.

And the majority of the time, she ran things with me. Most of the time, if she suggested that we do something, I would go along with it. Most of the time.

And that, again from my perspective, was the fatal flaw in our little slice of Heaven. Because, every once in a while, I'm going to stand my ground. And I think that can be difficult. What I often say is that I'm calm and mellow most of the time. But often people can mistake calm and mellow for dumb and, well, let's say cowardly. So when I suddenly show evidence of a backbone, it can take people by surprise. So every once in a while, when Cara would suggest something, I would decline. And again, from my perspective, it seemed to go like this;

"Let's go to dinner with the boys Friday"

"OK, cool"

"And Saturday there's a fundraiser in Irvine that I've got a table for".

"Great, sounds like a deal."

"Sunday we can stay at my house and make dinner".

"Actually, I'm going to take Sunday to get some things done."

"What things?"

"Things"

"Well, how long will these things take?"

And so on. Again, my perspective.

So, there was already some minor trouble in paradise when Ragnar So Cal came along. Cara told me that she was part of a team but I couldn't be a part of it because "We are a competitive team and have really fast people.".

Side note; One of Cara's big frustrations in our relationship was that she never beat me in any race we both ran. She was 10 years younger, and was a very competitive person. She would try to act like it wasn't a thing, but it was a thing. Ok, moving on….

So, I said "It's alright, I was asked to run with the team I ran with last year. No big deal". So we decided to run separately, meet up in San Diego at the end and go to a winery/ hotel in the area for the rest of the weekend.

I meet up with my team in Huntington Beach on Friday, early AM, and get started. Cara's team started later because they were faster as a team and the folks at Ragnar staggered the start times so that the teams finished more or less around the same time. So we're off and running. Another cool thing about Ragnar are the other teams you meet. You can use markers (non-permanent if you want the deposit back on your van) to write things on your van, get magnetic labels with your team name and "tag"other team's vans, etc. I met a team of hearing impaired runners from Denmark, all women. One of whom bridged the language/hearing barrier to outrageously flirt with me, tho of course I was in a relationship, so…

But you get the idea. Great fun.

So I do the 12 mile leg mid-afternoon and a 3-4 mile leg at around 1am. Now I have 1 leg left, at around 7am. I am stiff, sore, sleep deprived, smelly, etc. You know, having a ball. We are at the relay point, waiting for our runner #6 to show up (I am runner #7). When what team should be there but Cara's. They've caught up to us. Cool.

Now, one of the Ragnar things is "what runner are you"? Like I said, I was runner #7. Some of the runner assignments are designed for beginners, some for more experienced runners who can handle the distance. Cara had asked me what runner I was . When I told her I was runner #7, she told me about the 27 year old triathlete who they had as their #7 runner.

"OMG, he is SO fast. He's amazing".

"Umm, super. I'm very happy for him". Or something like that.

So, we are there at the relay point. Their #7 guy comes out to wait for their #6. Tall kid. Taller than me, and yeah, he looks like he's in great shape. I say "hi" . He says "hi". That's about all we got. Their runner shows up, they do the transfer and off #7 goes. Our runner showed up a few minutes later, we switch the slap bracelet and I'm off. It's about a 7 mile leg.

There is no way in the world I expect to see their runner again before the end of the leg. But around 4 miles in, there he is. Not limping or anything, just not going very fast, So, I pass him. And here is my thought process;

"Bob, you have run around 20 miles in the last 24 hours. You laid down in the back of a van, gotten little or no sleep. You are a leg cramp waiting to happen. Don't go crazy. BUT, for the rest of this leg, don't you dare go one second slower than you are able. NOT. ONE. SECOND.

And that's what I do. And I get to the end of the leg, which is a slow curved hill. And as I get to the top of it, I see teams waiting for their relay. And one of the 1st teams there is Cara's. And what did her face do when she saw me? Well, it did my heart good. It was one of the things I think about when I don't feel like going to the gym, or for a run. And as I run past them, to my team, I say to Cara "You and I both know what I am thinking".

That's it. That's all. But evidently, it was enough.

We get to the end of the run. we celebrate, take our group shot, clean off the vans and I say goodbye to my team. Cara's team is already there of course, having finished well before us. The plan is to ride in one of Cara's team vans to her car, which she brought to San Diego, then on to the winery and our weekend.

So after my folks leave I go over to her and her team & sit next to her. And get ignored for 30-40 mins. I'm sitting right next to her. She won't talk to me. She's talking to the boy to her right. I'm on her left. I try a few conversation starters. No response.

After, let's say, 30 mins, I get up and say "I'm going to take a walk". And that's what I do. Walk. And think.

I'm feeling like this non-conversation is a deliberate thing. I feel like I'm being punished. In front of 11 of her friends. And, in the interest of transparency, I'm also exhausted. And sleep deprived. And so my thought process goes something like this; I've already been punked in front of her friends. And according to our plans, I'm going to get in a van with some of these same people. And, as far as I know, I'm going to get punked again. For 30 mins or so until we get to her car. Then I'm going to get in her car and go to winery and spend the better part of 2 days with this person who seems to be really, really pissed at me. Is this my only option?

Tired or not. angry or not, I am nothing if not inventive. It occurs to me that there is an Amtrak train that runs from here back home to Orange county, close enough so that I can catch a cab from there to my place. So I continue walking. Out of the park to the Amtrak station where I buy a ticket for the next train to Orange county. While waiting for the train, my phone rings; "Where are you? We're leaving."

"Don't worry about it."

"What do you mean don't worry about it?

"Yeah. Well I've made other arrangements."

"What are you talking about?"

"I'm on an Amtrak train on my way back home.

"Is the room at the winery still reserved?"

"Nope. Cancelled it."

"Click". My next call was to the winery to cancel the reservation.

We communicated just once more. She asked me how soon I could get to her place and told me that my stuff would be on her porch. And that was that.

I miss Ragnar races. I haven't run one in a while. I'd love to put a team together again if the timing was right. I wish Cara well. I saw her at a race, with a new, very pretty boy shortly after the Ragnar. When I finished, I waited at the finish line, as I often do, and cheered people in. When she came along, her boy right along with her, I said "You go Cara!".

Her head didn't even turn.

I do appreciate consistency.

Ragnar running. Yeah, it's a kilt.

32-Barcelona & Star

I have to credit the company I worked for with getting me into the "travel to run" mode. They actually sent me to Barcelona to run my first full marathon. On 6 weeks notice. I had just run a half, but if you know running you know that that's not near enough time to go from 13.1 to 26.2 . But again , the Price Hill in me spoke up at that point. It said;

"Bob, people are offering to pay you to go to Barcelona, Spain to run a marathon. When you were 25, obese, and working as a receiving clerk in Cincinnati, did you even dream that stuff like would happen? Who cares if you're not trained? Who gives a flying &%#@ if you finish or not?". In case you're wondering, yes, I finished. In 3:54. With 2 cramped up hamstrings.

At one point I realized that I really enjoyed the whole "travel to run" thing. And it might be cool to start taking running vacations. Go somewhere, run a race and then hang out and explore. My 1st choice?

Back to Barcelona.

Because the part I didn't share about that 1st time in Barca was that I had almost no time to actually explore the city. So I wanted to go back and give myself more time. I looked up the Barcelona half marathon, which happens in February, booked the race, the flights and the same hotel I stayed in for work.

I told you that story, to tell you this story.

Which is actually 2 stories.

I'm complex like that.

After I booked the trip, I shared it on Facebook and a friend of mine responded to my post. A young lady whom I had cruised with before as part of a Singles cruise.

"You are going to Barcelona? On Valentine's weekend?"

It hadn't really registered with me that it was the weekend of Valentine's Day. But that's the way she put it.

So I responded; "Yes, the race is on Sunday the 14th. I get in on Friday and I'm hanging out til the next Thursday."

"I want to come meet you for Valentine's weekend. I'm not ready for a half, but I'm in London and I'll just fly over and we can meet up for the weekend."

Again with the Valentine's Day thing.

Ivy is actually a runner, and an attractive 30-ish, Eastern European woman. We had cruised in the same group several times, but I had never noticed any particular attraction. But she was asking me. and in her words, on Valentine's weekend . So I said "Sure, no problem. I'd love to see you." I told her when I was getting in and she booked a flight that arrived around the same time "so we can catch a ride from the airport together".

Next thing is, I've got a room. At a nice hotel. So, hell, let's make the offer.

"You know, I have a room at the Grand Marina, right down by La Rambla. You are more than welcome to stay with me. I'll make sure there are 2 beds and then you don't have to get a room." Yeah, I said it that way. Because that's what you offer where I'm from. You offer the "2 bed" option. That's how I roll, OK?

"That sounds great! I can't wait to see you!"

I contact the hotel and request 2 beds. They tell me that it's not a problem. "Just let them know at the front desk when you arrive."

Let's leave that story there for the moment.

I had one stop on my flights from L.A. to Barcelona. That stop was Dublin, Ireland. And when I board the connecting flight to Barca, a group of a dozen or so Irish folk get seated all around me. They have on matching running shirts & hoodies with "Star Running Club" written on them. And I have a ball listening to their thick, super-fast Irish accents as they are talking back & forth throughout the flight. I figure that they are there for the race, so as we are de-planing, I ask one of them "Are you all running the half Sunday?"

"Yeah, we're running the wee race, aye." I'm pretty sure they didn't actually say it that way, but every other sentence a Irishman from the North says is punctuated with a "wee" and ended with an "aye" so there a decent chance that at least one of them happened.

One other detail about that meeting. I'm a bald man in a sunny world, so I have hats. Lots of hats. And for a while I started collecting them. A style called porkpie is the one I think looks best on me so I have a few. Or a few more than a few. And I tend to wear them when I travel. So I had one on during this trip.

And we'll leave that story there for now.

I get off the plane, get my luggage and go to a meeting spot to wait for Ivy. About 20 minutes later, there she is. Lovely, like I said, a very attractive woman. So, we hug. Then she starts talking about all of the attractive men she saw on the flight. And how hot she thinks Chris Pratt is. And she thinks that all Spanish men are sexy. It takes me about 90 seconds to figure out what she is actually saying, though the monologue continues well into our taxi ride to the hotel.

OK. You're not here for that. With me. Got it. I'm not really sure why you ARE here, or why you needed to emphasize "Valentine's weekend" in our correspondence . But you're here. Fine. You're a nice person. Maybe it'll be fun to have someone to pal around with. So I adjust my expectations on the cab ride to the hotel.

When we arrive, I get to the checkin desk and request 2 beds in the room.

"I'm sorry sir. We are fully booked and you reserved a King room.that's all that is available."

She's right there. She hears it.

Again, my response is based on my upbringing. My Price Hill is present and accounted for.

"Don't worry about it. You're got the bed. I'll work something out."

Now, I said that. But my expectation was that she would say what she was "supposed" to say. Which was;

"No, we are both adults. we can share a bed. Just as friends. I mean, you're running a half marathon on Sunday. You need to get some good sleep." That's what I thought she would say.

I was wrong.

We get to the room. And it's a nice room. But like many European hotel rooms, it's fairly small. There's no couch. No comfy, small sofa-ish thing. There are 2 chairs, neither of which are suited to a 6'1" dude sleeping in. So where do I sleep? On the hardwood floor. With a blanket & 1 pillow. Friday and Saturday nights. Hardwood. Hard-freaking wood.

We go out both nights, of course. That was fine. Pleasant. On Saturday night we run into 2 French guys, nice guys, we hang with them until about 11-ish. I have to get up at 5:30 the next morning for the race. Ivy and the Frenchmen seriously ask "Do you really have to run tomorrow? We can just stay out and party".

I'm about done at this point.

"Yes. I really have to run tomorrow. You don't have to stop, Ivy. You can stay with your new friends. I'm leaving. Now." Like I said. Done.

As it turned out, she went back with me, I slept on the floor, got up at 5:30 and went to the race. When I got back, exhausted, sore and ready to fall down and sleep, did she want me to go out and sightsee with her because she was leaving that afternoon? Oh yes she did. And yes, I did. Because, well, I don't even know why. But I did. And when I walked her out of the hotel and into the cab to the airport that afternoon, I was ….

…jubilant.

I went upstairs and laid in the bed, fell asleep and had one of the best sleeps of my life. At least for the few hours I napped.

That's the end of that story.

Now, I woke up in the early evening, mostly because my body clock was still jacked up from jet lag. I showered and took a walk, because now I was free to do what I wanted. And I ended up in an Irish bar. Why an Irish bar in Barcelona? Couldn't tell you, but there I was seated at the bar, having a beer and celebrating the run and my freedom. Then I notice this guy, walking up to the bar. He's about my age, or at least close. And he's walking, well, like maybe he just ran a half marathon. So as he gets to the bar I said:

"Excuse me my friend. Did you run the race this morning?"

He looks at me, his face lights up and he says, in his thick Irish accent "You're the fella in the hat!"

Well, actually the word wasn't "fella" but it starts with an f and has the same number of syllables.

Dan.

He was one of the group on the plane. And he remembered the porkpie. The world is a funny place. So he being Irish and me being Irish-ish, we get to talking. About the race, about Barca, etc. And Dan noticed my Claddagh ring. It's an Irish wedding band, when worn on the correct finger on the correct hand. I wear it on the other hand as a good luck piece and tribute to my heritage... So Dan says;

" I see you're wearing the Claddagh".

" Yeah, my background is Irish and my Mom is way into her Irish roots"

" Oh, yeah, what's her name?"

"O'Donnell. Her family is from Donegal"

"Well damn! I've got an O'Donnell from Donegal over at the table!"

And so the Star Running Club from Derry, Northern Ireland adopted me for the next 2 days. They were, and still are, crazy, funny, positive and just amazing folk. When they get rolling I can't understand 1 word in 3, and they are amused at my "American-isms". As we were hanging out they mentioned that there is a race in Derry in September, the Waterside half marathon. Maybe I'd like to fly over and…?

I booked the flights, hotel and race before I even left Barcelona.

I've run, at last count, 4 Waterside halfs. Star Running club is my 2nd family and Derry is my 2nd home. Is Ireland as beautiful as they say? Sure. But it's the people. That's what brings me back, and has gotten me my Naturalized Irish citizenship. Thank you Grandpa Charley from the tiny town of Bruckless in Co. Donegal.

So that's the other wee story, done & dusted, aye.

Post race with Star Running Club. Derry, N.I.

33-Things I learned at the Horse Show

One of my "side-gigs" while I lived in L.A. was being an announcer at horse shows. Not Kentucky Derby type thoroughbred horse races. These shows highlight cow horses and their riders. They are judged on how well they work together, either on predetermined patterns or working cattle. It's way more complex than that, but that's the simplistic version, and also about as much as I really understand. There's a judge, a person to "scribe", or write down the feedback from the judge as the judge is focused on the horse & rider during the routine, and me, the announcer. They let me know via radio what the scores are and I in turn announce them to the audience. I also may, depending on which class is working, be timing them, announcing who's next, giving miscellaneous updates and information, etc. It's usually Friday through Sunday, 8am each morning until anywhere from 3:00pm to 7:00pm, depending on the number of participants. The gig is actually challenging because it goes basically uninterrupted, except for when they are switching venues or dragging the arena to even out the dirt. The moment I switch off, check my phone or try to get clever with someone around me, I will miss a score, not turn the timer on/off or call the horse or rider by the wrong name.

As I worked on a recent show, I started reflecting on what was going on around me and what my place was in this little world. My observations were, in no particular order.

-The group discovered that I can sing, so I occasionally sing the National Anthem before we begin. I'm reminded of when I used to sing in competitions when I was in college and often would have to sing early, like 7:55am. Singing early is its own challenge. And even though I'm just singing a cappella, for cowboys & cowgirls whose expectations are basically nonexistent, I still worry about it.

-When I get cold my nose starts running and it doesn't stop until long after I am back someplace warm. Which means my nose ran 9 hours Friday, 11 hours on Saturday and 7 hours on Sunday. That's a lot of tissue and one fairly sore nose. Also, I look SO good like that.

-There are lots of kids around, and I can't tell you how happy I am to see kids playing outside, in the dirt and mud .In this day & age of kids (and adults) permanently attached to their iPhones and gameboys, watching kids chase each other in rubber boots, make mudpies and splash through puddles does my old school heart good. And watching a mom take off her 3 year old's boot, pour the muddy water out of it and then put the boot back on and send her back out to do it again, made me actually laugh out loud.

I have maximum respect for all amount of work these folks put into their preparation for these shows. The relationship between horse and rider takes time to establish and can be fractured by the tiniest thing. And related to that, and this is something that I also learned when I was in the circus, The riders and trainers LOVE their horses. I know that some people have different and very strong opinions on this subject, but this is mine. It's a relationship. It's a love affair. It's a commitment and they have to contribute an amazing amount of time, effort and money to make that relationship work. Back in my circus days, I've watched trainers throw hands at each other over perceived mistreatment of animals, and watched trainers bawl like kids when an animal passed. You don't have to agree with that, but having watched it, that's what I believe.

These riders are in competition, but they are also incredibly supportive of each other. Most of the audience at the shows I do are other riders. They get scored and they get prizes, monetary and otherwise, but they are there to cheer and encourage each other. They don't have to be. And this weekend it was COLD people (have I mentioned that?) But they were there for each other. And I think that's pretty cool.

I have learned that horses have personalities. They are smart, and they will test you. I know this because I once tried to learn how to ride a horse for a Disney Europe audition. In 24hrs. Over the phone. I called my friend Kelley, who actually got me the horse show gig and is a rider and trainer. When I called her and asked if she could teach me to ride, she said

"Sure! Let's get together next weekend. I'll put you on one of my horses and we"ll start with some basics."

"Uh, actually, I need to know for tomorrow, for an audition. Can you tell me how, over the phone?"

Kelley laughed. A lot. Then gave me some basic instructions, which she told me would probably not work because "the horse will know."

The next day, that horse knew. I tried to do the things that Kelly told me to do. Tried to do them with assurance, as if I knew what I was doing. The horse basically turned it's head, looked at me, and starting wandering off in some random direction, with me on it's back, as I ineffectually tried using the reins and my legs to influence it, until the people in charge mercifully ended that travesty...

...but I digress.

And I am definitely not a cowboy. Not even close.

In a parking area full of trailers and pickup trucks, there was only one Mini-Cooper. I tried wearing a cowboy hat & boots the first time I worked a show. Kelley looked up from her desk, tried not to laugh, and told me that I might just want to go with my normal duds. During the shows, I've had riders hand me the reins to their horses while they go to the office, or the bathroom. I think I looked kind of like I would if Daenerys Targaryen were to hand me the reins to a dragon. Halfway between confused and terrified. And everybody wears boots and cowboy hats. Everybody. 2 years old to 92.

The point is, I don't blend. However, they have taken me in, Mini-Cooper and all. They appreciate what I do and how I do it. And I think that's very cool. I did the shows right up until I left L.A.

Never about the money. Again, it was all about the people.

B. Tully. Horse holder

34-Back to Cincinnati

Why back to Cincinnati? After 35 years of living in
L.A., with stops in the Caribbean, Japan, touring, etc. Why go
back? Good question.

I left my corporate job during the COVID years, like
many folks did. There were other factors, but basically, I
looked at my situation, looked at my finances , and put in my 2
weeks. What followed was a year off.

I did some background work. We've discussed that. I
did some performing, but nothing that was going to pay bills. I
looked into self-employment and other job opportunities. And I
enjoyed my break from the working world. But after a year, it
was time to make some choices. I had been good, money-wise,
while working at my corporate job. So there was a nest egg, but
not a "rest of my life" sized one.

I really do like L.A. I have a lot of friends there. I like
75 degrees and sunny. I like the diversity. I like really good
Asian & Mexican food. I like being able to run year round
without the ice, snow and runny noses. And being only 62 at
the time, going back to work on some level was a given. But
was there an alternative to Los Angeles?

That's where Cincinnati came in. I was raised there. Most of my family still lives in the area. I have friends and contacts from the 27 years I lived there. I came back to visit on a fairly regular basis. But, could I live there? I'm a big city guy, I admit it. Was there enough of that in my hometown to make me happy?

And…Cincinnati won. At least on a trial basis. The thought was, I could go back, get a small place and try life In Cincinnati on for size. Get a job, at least part time. See about reestablishing connects, both familial, personal and professional. So I found a little apartment in a part of town called Mt. Adams, packed my stuff into a POD, if you know what that is, got in my Mini-Cooper and made the cross-country drive.

And it's working. Not the way I thought it would, but in a totally different and interesting way. I've fallen into a performing arts opportunity that I didn't know existed. There is a lot of paid, non union theater on the east coast. I didn't know it existed, but it does. And guys "of a certain age" are not all that common. People my age don't necessarily want to travel, live in "artist housing" for weeks/months at a time and be away from home for extended periods. So I keep my place in Mt. Adams, travel 50% of the time and work in theater. It'll be interesting to see if this paid theater thing actually pans out as a long term thing. If you've actually read this far you'll realize that it's not the craziest idea I've ever had.

And so we move forward.

Home again, home again.

36-Accept the Gift

In my current job, we are often "dark" on Monday & Tuesday. We could just say we are off work, but in performing arts, everything needs to be different & special, so we say we are "dark". Whatevs.

So on this particular Tuesday, I went to the mall. Why the mall? Because on Monday I spent a fair amount of time at the pool. In the sun. In South Florida. And at one point I shifted on my deck chair and caught a glimpse of my skin just above & below my bathing suit. There was quite a difference. If I was a steak, I'd say I was medium well, on my way towards well done. Everyone knows that medium rare to medium is how you should have your steak, if it's a good steak. so....? I was overdone. Not badly overdone, but right on the border.

So no beach/pool time Tuesday. After my gym time and study time for the new show, I decided to hit the mall. Air conditioning, food court lunch, maybe pick up a thing or two. You know, the mall.

So I find the local mall on my GPS, head over and start my wandering. There was a book store, which was a great start. Had some acceptable orange chicken & white rice, cool. On my way over to the Macy's I saw this little shop called "Edison

& Ford". They carried antique and historic items and actually had an old Model-T car in front. They also had a piano in the store, with a woman playing. I noticed it because she was using an iPad for her sheet music, which I thought was pretty cool. So I wander the Macy's for a while, peruse some other stores, then head back the way I came. As I pass Edison & Ford, I hear that the woman is playing " Some Enchanted Evening" from the musical South Pacific. It being a classic Rogers & Hammerstein musical, I've done 3 productions of it, one as the character who sings this song. So I hear that she is playing it in the correct key, almost like it's from the score. I walk up to the entrance, where a gentleman who works there greets me. I return the greeting, but I'm really listening to the woman play, trying to figure out whether she's on the first verse going into the 2nd or the 2nd verse going into the bridge. That takes me just a second, then I simply turn towards her and start singing.

Why?

I'm not sure. You get a vibe about what's alright to do and what's not. My vibe, after about 10 seconds, was that it would be alright. So there.

The sales guy was, how can I say, sorta gobsmacked. He just said "well" and stared. But the pianist? She was a pro. she looked up, surprised, then looked back down, opened her ears, and got on with the business of accompanying her impromptu soloist, namely me.

How did it go? Actually, not half bad. I even liked the last note, which is always tricky because it should have a bassbaritoney quality to it, and my voice starts into more of a bari-tenor sound at that point…

…but I digress.

We finished the song, the 8-10 people who'd stopped by the door applauded, I turned to the pianist and said "Thank you". She said "No, thank YOU! What are you doing next Tuesday?" She was funny, this one. I wished them a good afternoon and walked out of the mall to my car.

A total interaction of maybe 90 seconds. But I was lifted. What is "lifted", you might ask?

Elevated. Mood lightened. Outlook on life improved. And it stuck with me for the rest of the day. I've been thinking about why this tiny, random event affected me so profoundly. The best I can come up with is….It was an unplanned, beautiful, fun, interaction with other folks, whom I didn't know, and we were all open to it. I can be closed, when it comes to my day to day life. I am comfortable on my own and I can wander around in my own little bubble, oblivious to the world around me. I think this was a reminder to me that people are kind, smart and giving, if you give them a chance. Something I need to do more of. Stay open to the beauty, grace and humor of the world and the people in it.

Just another life hack, from me to me.

36-Back to Work

Well, it's Thursday of closing week. "The Mousetrap" is the 5th show I've done since I got back to Cincinnati. Well, the 5th professional job. Like, for money and all. As I've stated before, I had no idea that this was going to become my "semi-retirement" job. I thought I would pick up something part time, and actually interviewed for a couple of regular jobs. I even taught a high school choir.

For 4 days.

I was naive.

I now have a new found appreciation for teachers...

...but I digress.

Back to "Mousetrap". I've got a show tomorrow, 2 Saturday and 1 more Sunday. Then I am heading back to beautiful Cincinnati, hopefully to enjoy my postage stamp of an apartment, La Rosa's pizza, Skyline chili, running down & up Mt. Adams, the river and all other things Cincinnati related. So what have I learned from this new job I've stumbled into?

And yes, I think learning is a big part of this work I'm doing. I'm doing shows with and for some very gifted, very driven people. A lot of these folks are hella talented, and have ambitions which reach as far as you can reach in this business. And some of them will be names you will get to know, especially if you're into stage work. Many of these people have made the move to the Big Apple. They aren't just sitting at home talking about it. They are being about it. All of this is to say that for me to belong on stage with them, as Ru Paul so elegantly put it, "I betta work".

Sometimes I wonder why I am putting myself through all this. It's not for the money. As I say to myself from time to time, I could make more working part time at an easy gig back in Cincinnati. Wake up, put my 20 hours a week in doing whatever, sleep in my own bed, have goetta & eggs whenever I want, ya know, the good life. By the way, goetta is a Cincinnati thing. Pork, beef, pinhead oats and spices. I actually made goetta over the holidays while I was doing "Christmas Carol" in Pennsylvania, enough to give to a few friends as gifts. "Here, have a loaf of goetta". Well, it's beef & pork and pinhead oats, onion & spices. Really. slice it up, fry it & have it with eggs for breakfast. We love it in Cincinnati. Let me know what you think".

They took it.

No response.

Yeah, I guess it's a Cincinnati thing…

…but I digress

So why travel all over the eastern U.S. To Florida, N. Carolina, Lancaster Pa. and who knows where else? In the words of Edmund Hillary, "because it's there".

Because I'm still learning. At 63. Trying to "up my game". Trying to be a better actor, singer, scene partner.

Learning how to keep my voice through lead roles and 7,8 or 9 show weeks. Learning about shows that I didn't know before, roles I didn't know before, theaters and actors and directors that I didn't know. I know that I'm good at being on the road. I can amuse myself, with the help of books, running paths, the internet, movie theaters, though don't get me started on the behavior of most people in movie theaters, or theaters in general. That's a whole separate rant. And the work is fascinating. I know it's not Broadway. But to be honest folks, this is as close to Broadway as I am likely to get. Every time I'm lucky enough to get cast and have the opportunity to work in this kooky business, I might as well give it my all. What in the bejeezus am I saving it for?

Has this work taught me anything? Yeah, I have learned a lot about getting out of my own way, not letting my ego and testosterone get in the way of doing good, sustainable work.

So, the point is that once again, I'm lucky. I've been put into a position where I get to do work I love with people who amaze, amuse & challenge me on a daily basis. And so I try to remember that,

...and appreciate it.

38-The Happy Ending

What is the happy ending to all of this?

Well, I think the happy ending is more of a happy continuance. And what have I got to be happy about?

-I'm not rich, but my bills get paid.

-I'm not married, but I don't think that was ever really in the cards. I think if I had done it, I would simply have an ex-wife or two and maybe some children running around. I am very content on my own, and need time away from even my best friends.

-I don't own a house, but I'm out of town about 50% of the time, at least, so I don't know who would be cutting the grass and getting the mail anyway.

-What I'm happy about is, well, being happy with me.

As I've mentioned before in these stories, I've worked with, and had the opportunity to meet and spend time with some amazing people. While being, at best, modestly talented myself. But knowing what I have done with the gifts I've been given, how far I have come from the painfully awkward teenager, the marginally talented performer who didn't know life outside of my own small circle. And knowing the work that it took, both physically and physiologically, to do some of the things I got the chance to do.

In writing this last piece, I recalled a phrase I have used as a mantra more than once, when life was challenging.

"Sometimes the only person who needs to believe in you, is you"

That phrase has gotten me through a lot. From Price Hill to Los Angeles, to the Caribbean, to Japan to Canyonville Oregon and a hundred places in between. All to come back to my home. And appreciating the Cincinnati of 2024, which is a far, far cry from the city I left in 1987. Not that I know it well. At least not yet. But I'm learning.

Back Home. Hudepohl 14k, Oktoberfest 2023

And Price Hill? I'm getting to know her again as well.

Goetta & eggs at Price Hill Chili, the fish sandwich at Jim & Jacks, tail-gating at the high school football game and a thousand other things and places I have yet to discover and re-discover. Though I'm currently living in Mt.Adams, Price Hill is 10 minutes from my front door.

But I think it's always been close by. Whether I'm in L.A., or Japan, or any of the far flung places I've called home. It's an attitude, or maybe a lack of attitude is a better way to put it. A way of dealing with life without the affectations, and treating everyone like you want to be treated. That's what I think has stuck with me throughout the years, the gift I've been given from growing up on Trenton Ave, just off of W. 8th, right down the street from St. Williams.

And something I will always carry with me.

THE END